HUNTING KILLERS

MARK WILLIAMS-THOMAS

CORGI BOOKS

TRANSWORLD PUBLISHERS
61–63 Uxbridge Road, London W5 5SA
www.penguin.co.uk

Transworld is part of the Penguin Random House group of companies
whose addresses can be found at global.penguinrandomhouse.com

Penguin
Random House
UK

First published in Great Britain in 2019 by Bantam Press
an imprint of Transworld Publishers
Corgi edition published 2020

A CIP catalogue record for this book
is available from the British Library.

ISBN 9780552176149

Typeset in 11.5/15.75pt Sabon by Jouve (UK), Milton Keynes.
Printed and bound in Great Britain by Clays Ltd, Elcograf S.p.A.

Penguin Random House is committed to a sustainable
future for our business, our readers and our planet. This book
is made from Forest Stewardship Council® certified paper.

MIX
Paper from
responsible sources
FSC® C018179

1 3 5 7 9 10 8 6 4 2

HUNTING KILLERS

www.penguin.co.uk

I have written this book to help those victims, and their families, who have been let down by the authorities and systems that are meant to protect and help them. To shine a light into the darkest of corners and bring attention to the many unsolved cases where families and loved ones still suffer without justice. It is to them, and to all the victims of crimes that remain unanswered, that this book is dedicated.

CONTENTS

Introduction

'BLOOD CRIES OUT FROM THE GROUND'

WHEN SOMEONE DIES, THEY TAKE THEIR SECRETS TO the grave. If the death involves a missing person, or a dead body is found somewhere, investigators – me, the police – start with this absence; we have to work back through the last days, weeks or months of this person's life. Piecing together half-remembered conversations from witnesses, where the victim went, who they saw, what they did. Slowly we assemble a mosaic of the life that's gone, witnessing their joy and their boredom, stepping warily through minefields of sexual desire, rejection, loneliness and unhappiness. Often we trace threads which unravel to nothing of consequence; but we always aim to tug on one that yields a result.

When a person meets a sudden, violent end, those closest to them – friends, family, colleagues – often end up learning more about the deceased than they might have liked. Much more, perhaps. The victim's private life gets laid bare in a way they probably wouldn't have wanted when they were alive. Some-times with good reason – their lifestyle may have been a contributing factor to their death. Their sexuality, the people with whom they mixed, the places they went, the drugs they consumed; they would have kept all these things to themselves, hidden from their families. These details, however – even if they weren't direct causes of a person's death – are all important parts of an investigation.

A case, for me, usually begins with the words: 'You're my last hope.' More often than not, it's the first thing I hear from a new client. For whatever reason, the police, the justice system, the authorities have all failed them. They've been let down.

I'm passionate about what I do. I believe in protect-ing the innocent, and tracking down, exposing and enabling the prosecution of the guilty. There are times when I probably have too many cases on my books, overloading myself and my small team, but I care deeply about trying to help those in need. I'm deter-mined to achieve the best result for all my clients. It's about giving people a voice and shining a light in the darkest of corners.

The highly sensitive nature of the investigations I carry out, as well as the absolute need to protect the anonymity of both my sources and some victims, has meant that in the past I've been reluctant to reveal how I go about what I do. I've felt, before now, that to give away how I track down witnesses and painstakingly follow clues could expose the very people I've promised to protect. When asked about my methods, I usually reply that my approach is delicate, sensitive and determined, but that I use quite simple investigative techniques. Now, though, I'm on the brink of an exciting development that will change the way missing persons cases and unsolved murders are handled in this country, and it's the right time to disclose my methods as part of this development.

These days I'm known mostly because of my TV show *The Investigator*. It was for a different series, ITV's *Exposure*, that I made a programme exposing the historic crimes carried out by the now widely discredited Jimmy Savile. The exposé laid bare to the world the extent of his abuse; but he wasn't the only individual to have acted in this way. Others did so, some of whom have also found themselves in court, after concealing their offences for years. As well as the stories of these individuals, there are plenty of crimes of other well-known figures – even if not everything they did is yet in the public eye.

I'm asked to handle investigations into all sorts of crimes and I'll consider taking on almost all of them – apart from medical negligence ones – although time and resources obviously restrict me. However, most of my work is taken up by missing persons investigations or unsolved murders. In many cases I've worked on, the crime in question took place ten years ago or more. On one hand, those can be the more challenging investigations (there's usually little or no CCTV footage to review, almost no social media to trawl through, and sometimes not even any forensic material to re-examine), but on the other hand they can be easier. Policing methods have changed drastically for the better in the past ten to fifteen years, meaning that any investigation undertaken into a crime committed before that time often has gaps in it that I can explore. Witnesses, constrained in the past by fear or misplaced loyalties, sometimes have different priorities a decade or two later, and are more willing to come forward and speak to me. For that to happen, though, they have to know that the investigation is still open and that someone is here to listen to what they have to say.

I receive so many letters and emails that I have to weigh up carefully which cases I can take on. One recent approach, for example, was a request for help in looking for a woman lost for nearly twenty years, the sender fed up with what they saw as a lack of interest from the police.

Another correspondent also wanted to find someone who'd been gone for a similar amount of time, only on this occasion they didn't think the police lacked interest, but money. The search they wanted me to undertake spanned hundreds of miles – from the east coast of England all the way to Portugal – and, according to them, had links to many infamous crimes from the past two decades as well.

A couple of others came from people wanting help in solving murders from thirty years ago, both in the UK and overseas; and yet another came from someone who served time for a crime but claims they were wrongly convicted – they want me to prove their innocence.

The sad truth is that I can't help them all, and the reasons for that vary. There might not be enough to go on. Or the crime might have been committed so long ago that the police have destroyed the evidence. Key witnesses may be long dead. Unfortunately, just as the police don't have the resources to take on cases that go on for twenty or thirty years, neither do I. I have to think of the people I do decide I can help, the cases I've committed to undertake. I can't spread myself so thinly that I end up doing a poor job for everyone. It's much better to do a good job for a few people. It's unfortunate, but that's how it is. There's only one of me, and I have to do what I think is best for my clients, my family, and for myself.

When I do consider taking on a case, I have to weigh up the difficulties it presents versus the benefits it might bring to the family of the victim. First, I make a quick mental assessment, from the moment the crime was discovered. Then, I ask myself what sort of access am I likely to get: who will talk to me, and will they talk freely? Will the police cooperate? Will the family cooperate? What information are they likely to give me? Especially with some of the older cases I'm asked to take on, if no one is willing to talk to me, I'm going to struggle from the get-go.

Finally, I have to ask myself, what can I do that will further the case? Can I realistically reach a conclusion? Are there lines of enquiry that haven't been followed up? And, most importantly, can I take it on without giving false hope to the victim's family? If I don't think I can make a difference, I won't accept a case. While I know I won't let myself fail, I do have to make sure I manage the expectations of the family and make clear to them the limitations of what's possible.

Right at the start I indicate that I will do everything I can to unearth more information for them. I never promise that what I find will result in a prosecution but, hand on heart, I can say that for every case I've taken on, I've always found new information.

When I started work as an investigator, one of the first assumptions I had to rid myself of was that the police had pursued every avenue in the original investigation. I learned quickly not to trust their efforts – not because I doubt what the well-trained and experienced rank and file officers would or would not do, but because I know that a senior investigating officer (SIO) leading an investigation will push resources towards the route that makes the best sense in an effort to solve the case. However, this can sometimes lead the investigation the wrong way.

From a policing point of view, I think ownership of the case makes a big difference, and in the police service there's far too little ownership of investigations. For every case with which I now deal, I have ownership. I give reassurances to the people with whom I'm working, to the clients I'm helping. I give my views in terms of what I can and can't do. In a police investigation, so many people are involved, each with their own responsibilities, and the senior officer is also in charge of a number of other cases. Something or someone is going to get missed along the way. There's less scrutiny because the officers involved are doing too many things at the same time. They're always juggling the books because policing these days is entirely reliant on finances.

I don't have to worry about that because compared to the police I haven't got the money to juggle things – I either get paid to do it, or I don't. In an official investigation run by the police, if there aren't the finances to make enquiries, it can't be done. Sadly, today, many police forces won't investigate a case now unless there's a suspect. Well, my old-fashioned view is that you have to investigate a case to get a suspect. Sometimes cases do come with suspects attached to them, but by and large that's why an investigation is undertaken – to uncover evidence. If we're saying cases should be closed down because there's no suspect attached, then the whole point of being an investigator, in my opinion, has been missed.

So, once I've agreed to take on a case, my first job when picking up the police files is to review them sceptically. What did the police do, I ask? Once an SIO has a theory about the type of person who committed the crime and why, then there is little that will shake him, or her, free of their beliefs. As a result of that, what does this show they didn't do? In cold-case files, this is the most vital part of my process. As well as being able to ignore the SIO's prejudices, the intervening years – never mind the improvements in police procedures and forensic techniques during that time – allow me some perspective and the opportunity to make an impartial assessment.

From there, it's straightforward. I never harbour any preconceptions about a crime or who's responsible for it – I go where the evidence takes me. From my perspective, there's no timetable urging me to come to a conclusion before something awful comes to pass; that's already happened. I can calmly take my time to weigh up what's been placed in front of me; and I can see easily who, or what, has been overlooked. Almost all crimes – whether murder, abuse, burglary or theft – are about access and opportunity. Who had access to the victim? Who had the opportunity? I'm less bothered about motive at this point as I don't find that to be the best tool in solving a crime; for me, understanding why something happened comes later.

In the cases that follow, I'll detail how I set about tracing suspects, linking disparate clues, and I'll disclose the tools I have access to which enable me to scour the darker recesses of the internet. I'll explain how I draw on the expertise of contacts I made during my years in the police force – contacts on both sides of the law. This includes the people who open doors that allow me to move forward in an investigation – something I wouldn't have been able to do during my time on the force; and I'll also reveal how I go about persuading individuals to speak to me when they would ordinarily stay silent. They believe that in talking to me they're not opening themselves up to prosecution – which wouldn't be the case if I were still a police officer.

With each investigation, there's a straightforward process in terms of where I want to get to, and I'll always have a clear idea of how to get there. I'm also good at thinking on my feet, though, so if something unexpected happens, I'll quickly come up with a response. I've got the advantage of having worked for the police, meaning there aren't many scenarios I haven't experienced before in some way – either in training, on the job or from my time as an investigative reporter. They all give me ideas to call upon to work out the best way to take action in any given situation.

One thing to note is that because I'm handling several cases at once – all of them at different stages – some of the stories I have to tell will be incomplete. That's the usual state of affairs for me, as some cases are never fully resolved. It's not always possible to get all the answers for a victim's family. The murderer might have been convicted of the crime, even have confessed to it, but they might never reveal where the body is buried or how they actually killed their victim. For the families involved, this can be heartbreaking.

This book is about my hunt for justice. In many cases, I'm able to help bring about a successful conviction. However, my job can also be to reveal the extent of criminal activity by someone who is yet to face court, who might already be in jail or (in a few cases) who might be dead. That then gives victims or their families the chance to speak up and be heard. For the victims of serial abusers such as Jimmy Savile or Max Clifford, that's extremely important – and not only to be heard but to be believed. For others, who've had to watch a trial collapse because of a failed investigation, I can perhaps help to find the new evidence that will finally bring about a conviction.

In every case I take on, I offer hope to the families. I manage their expectations about what I can deliver but I keep the promises I make to them. If someone's loved one has died a violent death, that's an incredibly shocking event that will have drawn the family, unwillingly, into a horrible and frightening world. It's a world I inhabit on a day-to-day basis, though. I've stood next to, chatted with, even had tea with some of the perpetrators of these terrible crimes. In the pages to come, I'll take you through some of these encounters. There's nothing to mark out any of these offenders as special. No unusual charisma, no dark aura, nothing to connect them, and certainly nothing glamorous. They're all just people – which is what makes them so hard to catch.

1

STARTING OUT

I JOINED THE POLICE SERVICE AT THE AGE OF NINE-
teen, after I left school. It wasn't a difficult decision – I'd
already worked as a special constable before I signed
up formally – but it wasn't an easy decision either. I'd
also been offered the opportunity to travel to New
Zealand to play semi-professional rugby for a team
there. I thought long and hard about it, and although
I still get great enjoyment these days from watching
rugby on the television to relax, or from going to see
my son play, I've never regretted my choice.

I was a quiet child. So quiet that my parents became
particularly worried about me and took me to the
doctor, who referred me to a specialist. I had speech
therapy for several years as they thought I couldn't
speak at all. I think I was just shy. I didn't really start
talking until I was six years old and I remained quite
an insular boy. When I look back at my police development file – part of the package of papers built up

during my time at police training college – one of the comments reads: 'He needs to get involved more, he's very quiet, probably the quietest member of the class.' Being part of the police service, and dealing with the sort of people I encountered on a daily basis, brought me out of myself, though, and I don't think anyone who knows me today would say I'm quiet. I'm always clear about what I think and understand of a case, so I'd venture that most of the people I come across would say that I'm strong-minded.

For just shy of twelve years I worked for Surrey Police. By the end of my time on the force, after I'd been made detective in my late twenties, I reached a position where I thought, 'Do I want to remain a police officer for the rest of my life, or shall I take a new challenge?' Policing had become very different from what it had been when I began my career: far less proactive and much more reactive (dangerously so nowadays). It was increasingly difficult to undertake investigations without burying myself under mountains of paperwork.

Early on in my career (in my mid-twenties) I became a family liaison officer (FLO), the main point of contact between the family of a victim and the senior investigating officer (SIO), and a role which quite often put me in a difficult position. Bear in mind the well-known fact that the majority of murders are committed by someone known to the victim, or even a member of their own family. Therefore, as the FLO, I was also covertly infiltrating the family environment to see whether or not the family had any specific information about the crime that they might be holding back from the SIO.

The big lesson for anyone who has to handle the aftermath of a criminal incident is to remember that both sides – both the offender and the victim – have loved ones who will be affected by what has taken place. Over the years I've dealt with many murder investigations, and each one almost always features the same scenario: sadly, both families get left behind. Sometimes we forget that it's not only the victim's family who feels the impact of the crime, but also the offender's, who might have been oblivious to the actions of their relative. Often, the offender leaves behind a mother and father, brothers, sisters, even children, when they are brought to justice, and it's easy for the police – for society generally – to lose sight of that. In a case I dealt with recently, the parents of an offender only found out their daughter was being charged when they watched the news on TV. That should never have happened. Police officers should relay those sorts of developments to the family face-to-face.

During my time on the force, Surrey Police shot and killed a man in Dorking who had threatened his girlfriend and was known to have a handgun. I was the FLO alongside officers from Hampshire Police who were investigating the shooting by Surrey Police (as was the way these investigations were conducted back then), and were looking after the victim's family. It was a particularly difficult posting because I found myself becoming incredibly sympathetic to the family, after seeing the effect it had on his children. It wasn't a case of me going native, but I did find myself asking questions about the circumstances. Was it right that their father had been killed? What follow-up procedures were established that would prevent those children feeling anger towards the authorities that had treated them with contempt – because that's what it must have seemed like to them? They weren't responsible for their father's actions, but people outside the family were acting as if they were. I had to be careful to try to stay detached – to be there for them, but not to collude with them.

I started my career in the police service with the intention of staying in the force for thirty years, expecting to leave when I reached the age of forty-nine and to live off my police pension. The reality of life on the job is different to expectations, though, and as time went on I started to think, 'Actually, I don't know if I can do this for the rest of my working life.' I'd been an officer for twelve years by that point, and I decided that it was time to move on and face other challenges.

I don't think I'm different from many people in that respect. Gone are the days when you take up a career and stay in it for the rest of your working life. People frequently move on to other jobs in different fields today; job titles you had no idea existed when you first started out become opportunities as you learn more and more about the world beyond your job. I think you can create your own luck: put yourself in the right place, and put yourself out there. Life's not easy, there are always going to be challenges, and you have to be prepared to meet them. We're all constantly reinventing ourselves too; what we wanted when we were twenty won't always be what we want when we get older. I don't believe key elements of your character change; when I joined the police service I wanted to help people, and although my title and status are somewhat different, that underlying impulse is still there.

I'd just left the police force (initially to learn business by shadowing former England rugby player Jeremy Janion) when I saw an article in one of the police magazines. It was from one of the better-known TV production teams who were looking for a police advisor for one of their shows. I contacted them and outlined my interest in the job, spoke about the few TV appearances I'd made during my time in the police – news broadcasts, missing persons appeals, that sort of thing – and laid on my media experience (of which I had very little) with a trowel. I was invited to meet the team, and I visited their offices a couple of times before they asked me to advise on a programme for Channel 5, a drama series called *Murder Prevention*.

I was excited by the opportunity but remember coming home after I'd been given the job. I sat at the dining-room table and thought to myself, 'What am I doing? How do I go about this?' The self-doubt only lasted a split second, though. 'Of course I can do it,' I reassured myself. 'It's just a matter of explaining what I already know about police procedures to people who don't have that information.' Those procedures were second nature to me, so it was easy to recall and explain them when I was on set, and what had at first seemed daunting quickly became enjoyable.

My initial role then extended into an advisory one on other TV crime dramas; shows such as *Waking the Dead*, *Wire in the Blood* and *The Inspector Lynley Mysteries*. At one stage, I probably advised on most – if not all – of the crime dramas being shown on TV, both BBC and ITV. Filming was a real eye-opener, watching how the production team adapted procedures and protocols that serving officers took as gospel, then either rewrote or ripped them up and used their own versions. I quickly learned to make sure the production team knew that, whatever changes they made, it was important that their version should be credible. If they made something too unrealistic, then the public would pick up on it.

Often, the team pushed those boundaries, but I held fast in my opinions. Seeing liberties taken with procedures I knew happened in a particular way for a particular reason got me thinking, and I began to seek out the writers directly, before the scripts were delivered and before filming had begun. 'Before you write anything, talk to me,' I said to them, 'because I can give you an overview in terms of how the police would do it.'

I thought it would be better if the shows were as authentic as possible, and it was much easier to make sure of that at the start of the writing process, rather than at the middle or at the end – it's difficult to change a script once filming has started. The writers welcomed my input – not least because it meant less work for them down the line.

Audiences, I think, find it more rewarding to watch something authentic on screen, and I liked that my job allowed me to influence the shows in this way. I advised on *Waking the Dead*, starring Trevor Eve, for six years, and it was an amazing programme to be involved with. The attention to detail the team brought to each part of the production – from the script to set design to casting – was phenomenal. I'm pleased to say that some of the storylines featured on the show were based on real-life cases I dealt with, which I suggested to the writers but details of which were obviously changed slightly.

I still enjoy watching crime dramas to see how the expertise of advisors is being used. In many shows, I can see where the two worlds of fiction and reality intersect – where the drama takes over from true events, and the actual facts underpinning the narrative, as it rushes to a conclusion.

The aim of crime dramas is similar to the programmes I then started – and continue – to make, such as *The Investigator*: to create something that gets the public talking. The challenges of the two types of programme are different, of course. Dramas are great because you can fictionalize the endings. Reality, however, doesn't always give you a resolution. It becomes even more difficult when you have a true story and investigation unfolding in real time – which is, of course, the principle behind the investigative programmes I make – as no one can write the ending before it's happened. That's where the challenge lies for me and my team: to make our shows entertaining, captivating, but above all accurate, from start to finish. With a multi-part drama you have a beginning, a middle and an end, and this allows you to create the pace needed for a TV series. Each episode can end with a reason for viewers to want to watch the next one. They usually know where their programme's ultimately heading, whereas I can't tell you, by and large when I start my programmes, what the end point will be.

Sometimes it's important that I can't tell you, because otherwise there would be no investigation taking place. And I can't always promise that we'll find out certain things along the way and that the ending will reveal a villain who will then get sent to jail. Not knowing what we'll find out, what it will tell us about the crime, or what the result of our investigation will be is hardly the most promising pitch to make to a TV commissioning editor, but that's the nature of what I do.

My career moved on to working more closely with Sky News and ITV News, mostly the ways in which they reported major crimes, but also providing leads and other routes for them to follow. From news snippets to more in-depth pieces, and everything in between. To do so, I worked hard at cultivating contacts in police forces around the country who wanted to see a fair representation of their work on screen. Their interest was in getting stories out there, on occasion to appeal for witnesses and the like, and to ensure that whatever was broadcast about a story happening in their region was accurate. I made it my business to speak to as many people as I could to ensure that there was always someone I could ask for information should I need it. It was from one of these contacts, in 2008, that I was able to hear of a fascinating case developing in Wales.

At the time, ITV had a strand in the evening called

Tonight, whose editor was Mike Lewis. I went to see Mike and said, 'I've heard about this shocking story involving a priest in Germany who's grooming a child in Wales. Only this child is not actually a real child, "she" is a covert officer, replying online to the priest who thinks he's talking to a child. I think what we should do is go to Germany and confront him.'

'Brilliant,' Mike said. 'Love the idea, it's really good.'

I saw my opportunity. 'I'd like to do it.'

He was a bit taken aback. 'Well, you can't. You're not a face on ITV. I'll pair you up with one of the reporters.'

I thought it was a reasonable response so I agreed – at least I'd tried.

The police were happy for us to go ahead, as they didn't feel their evidence was being taken seriously enough at the other end of the chain. I travelled with the crew to Germany to confront the priest, but the reporter with whom we were supposed to be working was still on another assignment in another country. He wouldn't be able to join us for two more days.

As soon as we arrived in Germany, the crew and I paid a visit to the police – to introduce ourselves for form's sake, and to tell the chief officer about this priest and who he was really talking to online. We explained that we wanted to speak to this guy, not just because of the online chat, but because he had revealed to the covert officer that he possessed child abuse material.

The chief listened to us for a while and then called in one of his subordinates. He showed the photograph of the priest we'd brought with us to his junior, and the officer recognized him. This was encouraging, I remember thinking: a police officer is on top of the offenders in his area if he can recognize one so quickly. The chief explained to him why we were there and the officer replied that he would look into it in a week's time. I hastily explained that we only had a day or so for filming before we flew home, and that we therefore needed to see him tomorrow.

The two German officers threw up their hands in horror. 'Oh no, we don't have the resources to do that. We can't go and do that so soon.'

In fact, despite what they told us, the German police did pick up the priest the following day. We had him under surveillance, so watched as they arrived, arrested him and took him away, but then returned him home on bail. They proceeded to raid his house and seize his computer, but that was the end of things, it seemed. Then, the most bizarre moment of our trip occurred. Right after the police brought him home, the priest climbed into his car and we followed him to an industrial estate. He met and spoke to someone there for a short while, before getting back into his vehicle and driving to an internet café.

The crew and I followed, and our assistant producer (AP) slipped into the café, booking a spot on a machine near to the priest to keep a close eye on him. The AP kept his phone on but in his pocket and spoke quietly to us: 'He's online talking to someone. Don't know who it is.'

'We've got to intervene,' I said to my producer. 'We've got to go and confront this guy now. I don't know who he's talking to at this stage – it could be this covert officer in Wales, but it could be another child. He's clearly been spoken to by the police today, and yet he's chosen to come straight here. He's desperate, and could be about to act in some way which might involve a child we can't protect.'

The reporter we were supposed to be working with was still on his way to us from abroad, so the producer put me on to Mike Lewis back in London.

'Mark,' he said. 'Are you up to doing this? Are you up to going to confront him?'

'Well, it's easy,' I said, reminding him of what I used to do as a police officer. 'It'll be no problem at all, I'll just have a chat with him.'

Mike gave his permission and the crew and I moved in on the internet café, in what would be my first TV appearance on an investigative programme. The priest looked understandably shocked as our British crew entered the room, lights and cameras in his face. He looked like a rabbit in a car's headlights, but I got him to focus his attention on me. I spoke directly to him and surprised him by telling him we knew who he'd been talking to online – then startling him further by letting him know that it wasn't a young girl after all, but a covert officer. In the end he stayed and spoke with us for a while, telling me everything. He described his sexual interest in children, what ages he was interested in, and attempted to explain his behaviour.

If I'd have been a serving police officer, such an encounter would have finished with me arresting him. However, not only was I abroad, but I was also just a journalist. All I could do was urge him to go and seek help to deal with his inclinations – and hope the German police kept a close eye on him.

We spent nearly thirty minutes with him in the end. I suppose I'd expected him to run off as soon as he saw us, but sometimes when you confront people in that manner, they open up and talk to you. The strangest thing was, once we'd finished filming and I'd said my piece to him about looking for help, he went to leave the café. On his way out, he said to the guy behind the desk, 'How much do I owe you for that?'

'That's quite a strange thing,' I thought. 'He's just been bubbled by us, he's now going to be on TV around the world, and he's worried about paying for his time on a computer.' It was as if the previous half an hour hadn't happened.

That broadcast was my break into fronting TV programmes. I'd appeared in front of the camera, and that meant the reporter they'd planned to use was no longer an option. I'd carried out the confrontation, and because I'd done all the follow-up it became my gig. From that point on, I began to front more programmes, starting with other episodes of the *Tonight* strand. A *Tonight* highlight for me was a particularly important broadcast we did on the murder of Tia Sharp by Stuart Hazell (see Chapter 3). After that, I worked on the series *Exposure*, which culminated in the Jimmy Savile exposé. From there I moved on to *The Investigator*, a prime-time ITV series airing at 9 p.m.

I'd left the police to have more control over my hours of work, only to find myself busier than ever. However, I have more choice in when I spend time at home these days. Luckily my wife, who was also in the police, is understanding. We have three children – two girls and a boy. None of them has shown any interest in following their parents into the police, although our middle child, who's studying engineering, does show an interest in true crime shows on TV, watches everything I do on telly and talks to me about what's going on in some of my cases. The oldest works in structural engineering and our youngest is planning to study sports rehabilitation at university. They're level-headed, sensible, hardworking kids – all of which is down to their mother, of course.

They've had to put up with a lot. What I did before, when I worked in the police, was all-consuming, whereas now it's become more nebulous. 'What is it you actually do, Dad?' they used to ask me. Given that a large number of fathers leave the house for a 9 a.m. start and get back after 5 p.m. – regular hours for a regular office job – what I do must seem a bit, well, loose, given I do so many different things, often on an elastic timetable. Sometimes I'm kicking my heels at home, other times I'm abroad for a week. I'd have to repeat to them that, no, I was no longer in the police and, no, I wasn't doing undercover work. Yes, I was investigating, but not for the police any more.

I've always worked hard, and sometimes the kids have found that difficult. During the course of the Tia Sharp investigation in 2012, I was taking them to the theatre on a day off. As we arrived in London, my phone rang and I had to take the call. As I answered, my other phone went off. I told my younger daughter to pick it up, ask whoever was calling to hold the line and let them know that I'd be with them as soon as possible. When I finished the first call and switched phones, the BBC producer on the other end laughingly told me that my daughter had firmly but politely informed her that we were on our way to the theatre and that she shouldn't hold me up as we had a show to get to. It was nice to hear that my daughter wanted to make sure I didn't spend any more time away from the family than I had to.

I don't tend to talk to my wife about what I'm working on. Very, very occasionally I might mention that I'm finding something quite tough to deal with, or that there's a person involved in a case who I find hard work. I might even say that some of the stuff in a case is particularly horrific – but she doesn't ask if I don't bring it up first. She knows what the job's about, and how much I can and can't talk about.

The terrible, unconscionable things I come across, though, are rarely new to me – I saw plenty of horrible things when I was a police officer. Every element of murder and death you could think of: dead children, people who've been shot, people who've been stabbed, people with their brains hanging out. I've been to post-mortems carried out on babies. I've spoken to people who've suffered the most appalling abuse in their lives, and I've had to watch videos of the worst kind of sexual abuse of children.

I try not to let that kind of work intrude on my home life that much. It's impossible to separate the two worlds completely but it's important not to let the lines become blurred. The need to keep them apart is vital. If I didn't, then I'd never switch off. I work hard to make sure that they don't overlap and this helps: I don't have any trouble sleeping. I've always slept well; in fact, I don't lie awake, staring into the darkness, my mind racing. It's as if my body and my mind know I need to rest, so off I go, and they don't stop me.

Since changing careers, I've been able to devote more weekday hours to being with the family. I try to take Wednesday afternoons off, especially during rugby season – and if my son's playing a match at a local venue, then I'll go and watch. If he's not playing, or it's the off season, then there's usually something to do around the house, or I'll go and pound the tread-mill in the gym to clear my mind.

When I was working full time in the police, I'd go for a drive on Sunday mornings for the same reason. I still do this, though less often. I used to have a nice old Porsche; now I have a motorbike. Having to con-centrate on driving for an hour or so was – and is – a good way for me to empty my head for a while. It relaxes me. There's something about having to focus my mind on the present, having to switch off the con-stant chatter in my head about cases, clues and leads. If I'm not driving, then I like to get out in the garden, digging, weeding, dead-heading and pruning. Put like that, it sounds a bit like more police work, but it's another thing I find helps with my thinking time.

I don't tend to read much at home, I find it easier to listen to audio books in the car while I'm driving. When I was younger, I was diagnosed with severe dys-lexia, but I don't think you'd know that from the programmes I make and the things that I do. I've put some support systems in place to enable me to deal with it.

My dad does a lot of proof-reading for me, for instance. It was with his help, checking what I'd written, that I was able to get a master's degree in criminology – which I'm especially proud of, considering I left school with almost no qualifications. I also have a full-time PA who looks after all of my work, so I can dictate documents to be typed and proof-read. With their help, I write a lot for newspapers.

Having worked so hard to overcome the challenges dyslexia presents, I love it when I'm invited to schools, colleges or universities to give talks to students. My journey from being a man who always thought his career lay in sports or front-line policing, to finding myself doing the work I do now, has been an interesting one. I try to make the speeches inspiring, and say to my audience (and indeed to anyone out there who might be interested) that if you're struggling with something that could potentially hold you back in life, such as dyslexia, think about how you can meet it as a challenge, own it and actually work with it. In my case that's taking advantage of dictation software, putting in place somebody who does my typing for me, and having someone I trust to do my proof-reading. I'm incredibly lucky in this respect, I know I am. I'm also incredibly grateful, and I make sure to tell my audience that. I explain that it comes down to having a determination to get things done, which helps overcome those obstacles.

What is at the root of my determination? What drives me? What made me want to work in the police in the first place and then to carry on with investigative work, dealing with the after-effects of the worst of humanity? The answer's simple – I ask myself, what can I do to fix this? *Can* I fix this? Can I do something that will help? Can I get answers for the family involved? I ask them to offload their grief on to me – I'm quite good at handling it and I'm used to it. Being responsible for it gives me a focus, and motivation, that I can use when I come face-to-face with some truly awful people.

The disconcerting thing is that these people are never openly vile in public. They walk amongst us, concealing their true nature for the most part, but they don't bother me. I don't sit and dwell on them and what they've done. As soon as they're caught and convicted, sentenced and locked away, then I forget about them. Best thing to do.

None of the awful stuff I've seen sits in my head either. I can recall it if I have to – if I'm questioning someone, or if I have to recount something – but it's important that someone looks carefully at evidence, even of the most horrific in nature.

The vile recordings made of abuse is one example. There was an awful case a few years ago involving two men in a nursery in Spain who videoed themselves abusing the babies in their care. I wasn't involved in the case, but a reviewer of the videos spotted a ticket in the background. Through a careful process of identification they connected that ticket to a French Métro journey and then to a specific station on a specific day. On another still from the video, there was a guy wearing a top with a particular motif, and it was possible to link it to a garage near the Métro station. It transpired that one of the staff at the garage was the partner of the person carrying out the abuse, which led to the pleasing result that Interpol were able to make arrests.

The people whose job it is to review this horrific material, usually police officers, know just how awful it is. They are also trained to assess the whole image – all the details that fill the background, clues as to where the photograph has been taken, or the video footage filmed. This is done not only to try to catch the offender but also to try to identify the child so as to remove them from harm.

Everyone handles the emotional fallout from having witnessed something awful differently. When I was working in the police force, a protocol came in towards the end of my time. If we were dealing with a murder case, officers were required to attend a counselling session before being allowed to move on to the next case. Mostly we regarded it as an excuse to have a half-day off, drink some tea and eat some biscuits. I can't say I found it much use when I happened to be working on three or four open murder investigations at the same time – I felt I had to rush in, sit down and get my bit of counselling over so I could start looking into the next case on my list.

These days talking therapies are standard practice in most industries where employees have encountered trauma. Even today, when I'm working outside the police service as an investigative journalist. During the making of the Jimmy Savile documentary for ITV, we were all offered some counselling. I didn't take up the offer but I know some other members of the team did, which wasn't surprising as it was the first time they'd come across that kind of stuff. I've never felt the need to go and talk things over with a counsellor – not because I think I'm somehow immune but because I don't feel I need to right now. Perhaps in the future I will. At the moment I find my natural human reactions of rage and disgust are a driving force for me, and I don't want to lose that.

The horrific nature of some of the things I've dealt with makes me more determined than ever to try to find answers – especially for parents whose children have gone missing. There are a lot of cold cases from the seventies, eighties and nineties. The number of unsolved murders is difficult to estimate as there are, believe it or not, no official figures that cover all UK police forces. At present, estimates range from 1,500 to 2,300 but it could be five times that if we were to include all the people reported missing.

Not all unsolved missing people cases are murders,

which is why they're not included in the statistics. When the police started to unearth Fred and Rose West's victims from the cellar of the house in Cromwell Street in Gloucester in the early 1990s, they struggled initially to identify the bodies they'd found because it transpired there was no complete national register of missing young people. At the time the Wests began their protracted spate of assaults and killings, missing girls weren't habitually reported on a national basis. If they were in their late teens and disappeared from home, the police would often tell their families not to worry and that their daughter would show up at some point. That mindset has changed massively since then.

Unless there's a body, a case tends to stay on file as a missing person – but I suspect there are many bodies or remains buried around the country. Consider the case of the serial killer Peter Tobin. Following Tobin's conviction for the murder of Angelika Kluk in Glasgow in 2006, police searched his former home in Margate, 450 miles to the south. The bodies of two young women, previously believed to be missing but who actually had been killed fifteen years previously, were found buried there. How many others might he have killed? In 2017 I was asked to track down a missing woman, Louise Kay, and I believe she was one of his victims. I found evidence that another, Jessie Earl, might also have been killed by him (see Chapter 9). Are there others?

When I meet the families of victims such as Jessie Earl or Louise Kay, I find it hard to remain unmoved. The heart-breaking stories they have to tell, the frustration stemming from decades of what feels to them like official indifference to the death of their child, the awful thought that they will die with their questions still unanswered – those are the moments that can bring a lump to my throat and I'll become upset. I won't cry, because that doesn't help the family, but my eyes will fill. I have my own private motto, something I call to mind whenever I take on another investigation: treat every case as if it were happening to your own family.

It's when I walk out of one of these meetings – back on to the street, into a coffee shop or a supermarket – that I wonder how many people who have walked alongside us, have held open the door to let us pass through first, or have smiled as they hand over something we've dropped, are actually murderers?

2

THE INVESTIGATOR

MY WORK AS AN INVESTIGATOR TAKES ME ALL OVER the UK but also to far-flung corners of the globe. I welcome the challenge of working in new environments, dealing with different legal processes and different approaches to policing. The most complex situations arise when I'm working and filming abroad and engaged in something that might be – under the laws of the land I'm in – on the border of what is legal. It's not about me in those instances, but about the crew I'm working with, as I feel a huge sense of responsibility to ensure none of them falls foul of the law. I wouldn't want them to end up in jail because of something I overlooked.

I can rely on contacts a lot when I'm in the UK, but there's something exciting about being on my own when we're overseas. There's no safety net, no one I can call to say, 'Help me fix this, will you?' The greater the challenge, the more I want to take it on; when someone tells me I can't do something, or that it's not possible, I'll look very carefully. If I can see a little chink, I'll do it. Some things are obviously very difficult indeed, but I'll give it a bloody good go. You never know how it's going to end, and in the case that follows, things certainly didn't end the way we expected.

I'd been approached because two long-standing unsolved murders were being reviewed, and my team and I had received a tip-off from a retired senior detective that the chief suspect in the case was now living abroad in south-east Asia. It was suggested that if DNA from this suspect could be obtained – and then checked against DNA records on file with the police – the offender's identity might be confirmed. If that was the case, a warrant for his arrest would be issued, and extradition proceedings from the country he was living in would be started. If it proved otherwise, then at least he'd be ruled out as a suspect.

It was too early in the process to involve anyone outside the immediate investigative team but we were there at the start. If the evidence went the right way, we'd have the makings of a great TV programme.

I'm familiar with the guidelines governing the collection of DNA in the UK, but at the time I wasn't clear what rules applied when it came to obtaining it from someone when overseas, especially if – as would be the case for us – we were going to have to retrieve the sample covertly, without alerting the suspect.

DNA can be collected in this way in the UK, under the Human Tissue Act 2004, provided the sample collected is used in the prevention (or detection) of crime. Given that we were trying to help solve two murders, what we were seeking to do would be acceptable under UK law – but in an overseas jurisdiction, potentially less so.

For a start, there is the issue of theft. If, for example, we were to take a coffee cup from a shop or a glass from a pub in the UK, in order to obtain DNA from it, it's unlikely the issue of theft of property would arise. However, I had no idea what the situation was like overseas. What would be considered a safe and legal approach in a similar set of circumstances?

An additional concern, one which we knew how to work with in the UK but were uncertain about in other countries, was the issue of privacy. Would it be legal to take something from an individual in another country without their knowledge? What might be the consequences if we were caught? Not being clear on these issues – but not wanting to alert anyone unnecessarily by asking the relevant embassies – had the potential to land the team in jail. We would have to tread especially carefully.

There was yet another problem, one that would hardly feature in a travel guide but which we were likely to encounter: corruption. We couldn't risk doing anything that might leave us exposed to corrupt police officers, because we had no idea of the consequences we might face. Spending time in an overcrowded, squalid and dangerous south-east Asian prison was not what anyone in our team had signed up for, so I had to make it clear to everyone involved that we wouldn't do anything that might put us at risk of being considered a threat by the police – or by the suspect, who must never know we were even in the country.

Firstly, before we even left the UK, we had to be sure we'd identified the right man. I employed a private detective in the region, who found our suspect and 'housed' him – that is, clarified where his permanent home was in the country. We knew that the suspect was retired, but we had to find out how active he was in the community – did he get out, where did he go regularly, might we be able to get DNA from him when he was away from his house?

Once these basic facts were established, we had to plan as best we could what approach to take. We started to fill in a picture, using the information supplied by the PI as well as what we could gather online, of the sorts of local places the suspect frequented: bars, restaurants, that sort of thing. We looked at access points, roads, hotels, and all the stuff that you might normally research before you visit a place on holiday – how do I get to the beach, where's the night-life? Only this time we were on the search for DNA, not relaxation.

The obvious routes to take were the ones we'd already ruled out. We could have got his DNA from a coffee cup at a café possibly, or from a drinks can at a bar, but as it turned out the suspect never left his house to go to places such as that. We couldn't enter his home to take samples from his toothbrush or hairbrush either, as we knew that whatever we managed to obtain had to be done so legally – we couldn't use a method that would undermine the DNA we obtained. It might be all right if I decided to take the risk for myself, but I couldn't take the risk that my AP or the cameramen who came with us might end up in jail.

The next step was to speak to a UK lab offering DNA testing, to understand how we had to store and transport any material that might provide a sample. There we ran into yet another difficulty. Most of the labs we spoke to only worked with the police, and certainly weren't prepared to assist us if we obtained the sample covertly. I was a bit disappointed by this – we might not be the police but the purpose of our trip to south-east Asia was to confirm or eliminate a suspect in a murder investigation. Eventually we did find a lab that was happy to work with us, and willing to provide the information we needed to store and transport anything we wanted testing.

When it comes to obtaining DNA to be used as evidence, there's an additional level of complexity, which is to do with something called continuity. Essentially, it's about keeping the DNA material sterile, with a clear, visible and verifiable chain of control, from the moment it's identified through to the point at which it enters a lab for testing.

Let's say you're in a bar. You drink from a glass, which now has your saliva on the rim, so there's plenty of material from which to extract a DNA sample. However, to be sure it's your DNA, I would need to know first that the glass had been cleaned thoroughly before you drank from it. I would need to know that at no point had anyone else touched the glass, especially with a finger they'd just used to rub their eye, poke their nose, scrape a tooth, or whatever. Then I'd need to know that cross-contamination hadn't occurred from it being picked up by someone else, a waiter perhaps, and pushed next to other used glasses. Or that it had not been washed in boiling water before it could be taken. It's vital that the DNA remains uncontaminated and intact from the moment you drank from the glass, is isolated and bagged almost immediately, and is stored at the correct temperature right through to its arrival at the lab.

You can see the myriad challenges presented to us here. Leaving a DNA sample outside in a hot country would be a sure-fire way of corrupting it. From the first person seizing the item there has to be continuity, a chain of command from the moment the sample is taken, a chain that is not broken at any stage.

On this job, continuity meant being able to ensure that we saw the item we were going to use for obtaining the sample and kept sight of that item, certain it was never handled by anyone else. We'd need to have a camera filming the whole time to back up this process, right until we took it out of a cool box at the lab. It's not only about knowing we've got the item, it's also about making sure it's visible to a camera at all times, until it's sealed and tagged.

It's all very well if you're collecting DNA in a more conventional way, asking for a mouth swab at a police station, say, and bagging and tagging the sample on the spot. But covertly, in a street in a foreign city, outside a crowded bar? I wasn't sure how we were going to achieve this.

We ran into further difficulties before we even set foot on the plane – I realized I was going to have to find a new local investigator. One of the troubles with working from such a distance is that it can take a while before you discover you've hired someone with the wrong experience and expertise to carry out the job you're lining up – and that was what happened in this instance. Although the original PI had been able to get some basic information on the suspect, we were knocked back in our efforts to have him followed to see what sort of routine he kept and what kind of background information could be gleaned from those he spoke to or interacted with.

In the end I found a brilliant PI to cover these tasks. He spoke fluent English and worked alone, which was useful as I knew that if I asked him something there'd be no misunderstandings when the information was relayed. He could call upon a few people he trusted, though, who would help him do some of the leg-work – following someone and speaking to people along the way, for instance.

He was soon able to give us a rough idea of what the suspect's day-to-day activities were. Once we had that information there was nothing left to do except to get over there and try to get his DNA. The four of us – the assistant producer, two cameramen and me – flew in and drove for three or four hours to a hotel near (but not too close) to the suspect. We met with the PI and carefully visited the places we could observe our man.

On the first day of surveillance, the suspect stayed in his house – the local PI had confirmed he was in – and went nowhere. We sat near by in our cars in the muggy heat and sweated to no purpose. Two cars, with the PI and some of his locals sat inside, were close to the address while our two vehicles were parked a little further away. The local guys had walkie-talkies so they could give a full running commentary on the comings and goings from the house – of which there were far too few for my liking.

The second day came round and I began to feel a

little anxious. We only had seven days in all before we had to be back in the UK, bringing this man's DNA with us. I had to start to consider ways we might obtain a sample if he didn't leave his home. Legal ways, of course. Then, at lunchtime, the suspect emerged from his house and climbed into his car. We immediately set off, leaving a considerable distance between us and the group of vehicles in front – the suspect's and the two cars carrying the PI and his local crew.

The vehicles were crawling down the absurdly busy streets closer to the centre of the town, when the suspect's car pulled over abruptly. He parked up and hopped out. The PI spoke to me on the walkie-talkie: 'He's going into the dentist. He's stopping outside and taking off his shoes, he's got bare feet, he's heading inside.'

This might be our moment. 'OK, got that. Send in one of the guys to wait inside, keep an eye on him. We'll be right there.'

Hastily, I opened the browser on my phone and typed in 'can you obtain DNA from inside someone's shoes?' The clear answer that came back was yes.

'Right, let's go,' I said, and the car I was in raced forward as fast as the traffic allowed. As soon as we came to a stop, I grabbed some surgical gloves and a mask, and jumped out.

The local guy inside the dentist's was still keeping an eye on the suspect. He reported back that he'd gone into the dentist's surgery now, so I knew I had a little bit of time. How long, I couldn't be sure, so I had to act quickly. The PI pointed out exactly which pair of shoes I needed to pick up – they weren't hard to identify, really, as I'd seen them on him in the photos the PI had snapped and texted to me as the suspect left the house a short while ago. Wearing the mask and gloves to prevent cross-contamination, I scooped up the shoes and ran back to the car. I quickly swabbed their insides, dropping each swab into a separate sealable bag on to which I'd already scribbled the date. Each shoe swabbed thoroughly, I got back out of the car, darted across the road, replaced the shoes, and returned to the car. We drove around the corner and parked up, waiting to see what happened next.

No one in the street blinked an eye. No one said, 'Hey, what are you doing?' No one took out their phone to film this foreigner in a mask acting bizarrely, picking up some old shoes and racing across the street before dashing back to replace them.

All in all, it wasn't a bad effort and we had continuity. The suspect had been seen to take off his shoes – someone had watched and filmed them the whole time until I picked them up. My crew and I wore gloves and masks the whole time, so there was no chance of cross-contamination from any of us. Even though we couldn't control the environment, the continuity was there, so it wasn't a bad result.

As soon as the suspect came out to get into his car, the local guy waiting inside went into the dentist's surgery to grab whatever he could – mouth swabs, tissues, anything he could lay his hands on. He managed to get to the bin just as it was about to be emptied – he made up some excuse, took out the contents and bagged them. Good thinking from him, and potentially useful back-up if we hadn't succeeded outside, but there was an obvious problem with what was in the bin – the continuity was lost. We had no sight of the suspect while he was in the dentist's chair and no idea if there were other peoples' items in the bin, or if it was all his.

Day three rolled around. We still needed a better sample; something we knew was not contaminated by anyone else's DNA in any way. No opportunity arose; the suspect remained inside his house the whole day and evening. We got to know every bit of the inside of our little hire cars, in which we sat and roasted.

Day four. I'd finally come up with an approach we could try. Having worked in the police for such a long time, I know people in the same sort of business as me in lots of places. People with either a policing or security background; sometimes with a connection to me in the UK or, as in this case, someone I'd been put in touch with by a friend back home who vouched for me. I explained what my team and I were doing, and how I would appreciate some help. What this contact and I agreed, after a chat on the phone, was that he would call our suspect, explain that he'd been given his name by a friend back in London and invent some reason to be asking for our man's advice. He'd suggest meeting over a drink and a meal, and that would be the opportunity we needed to get him into a public space we could control.

I left this guy to make contact, and went to scout a restaurant where we could regulate all the comings and goings and place the team strategically around the suspect's table to ensure continuity over the items the two men would eat and drink from.

We found a perfect place, one which suited our needs and which would not have seemed an odd choice to the suspect. We ate dinner there ourselves that evening, and discussed how we wanted to lay things out for lunch – where our team would sit, where we'd put cameras, how we'd remain as discreet as possible. We also spoke to the management that night and explained that we were working with a very important man who had serious OCD – obsessive compulsive disorder – and we wondered if they could accommodate us. We told them we wanted to provide our own plates, glasses, cutlery, cups and saucers, and that we'd clear the table afterwards – not the waiting staff – and we'd also take everything away with us.

The restaurant didn't bat an eyelid – everything we proposed was fine with them – so our next task the following morning was to buy two sets of everything we'd need and prepare the table for their arrival.

I'm often asked why people go along with the odd things I propose, and it's always the same reason: my confidence. The bolder you are, the more people seem to accept what you're doing. I've been quite brazen in the past but if you do everything with an air of confidence, people will most likely let you get away with it. I tell my team: if you act like you're a bit nervous about what you're doing, or if you're a bit shy when you approach people to make your request, they will see through that. Don't be aggressive, but don't give them a chance to disagree with what you're proposing – they might think you're a bit weird, but they'll likely go along with you and allow you to do it.

Lunch between our suspect and our contact would take place on day five, so the team and I spent that morning covertly setting up some static cameras. We also made sure that the table next to theirs was occupied by a couple of locals from our team – two women who could keep an eye on things without being conspicuous. Another two team members would be sat near by – one of our cameramen and another local – with a camera positioned to keep the suspect in view at all times. Before the pair arrived, our team walked though how things would go – what would happen when the two men arrived, what to do if the suspect left the table, walking them out of the restaurant at the end of the meal so as to make sure they left before we rolled into action. It's always good to be prepared by rehearsing everything, because even if I think I know what's going to happen, you can't guarantee everyone on the team is on the same page as well.

Finally, just before the pair turned up, we took out the pristine plates, cutlery and everything else we'd bought earlier that day, and laid the table ready for lunch.

I sat around the corner with another of the cameramen, who was keeping an eye on the static cameras. The whole place was ready and we were covered in terms of the continuity element as well as footage, should we need it. We were good to go.

The two men walked in and took the table we'd prepared. Lunch lasted about an hour. There was only one moment when I thought things might go wrong, when one of the waiting staff cleared the plates. She'd been asked not to, but it was an instinctive move by her. We jumped into action immediately. One of the team stood up and shadowed her as she came in my direction, to keep an eye on the plates at all times. As she came near me, in my hidden position around the corner, I stood up and, with a gloved hand, took the plate off her and bagged it immediately. The expression on her face was clear. 'What on earth are these foreigners up to?' would be the polite version.

Lunch, beer, coffee. Fork, spoon, glass, cup. Once

finished, one of the team followed the pair out of the restaurant, as planned. We also had someone follow the suspect back to his home address to make sure that he appeared none the wiser about the set-up.

Wearing my gloves and mask, I made my way to the empty table and sat down. I set about putting stuff into bags, scraping off any leftover food (with a different knife) and drying any liquid in the glass and cup with a little bit of tissue first. I secured ten items in all.

We drove back to our hotel immediately, making sure that everything was being filmed for continuity. We'd had a lockable fridge, purchased locally, installed in the room. It was to be used only for the exhibits, and once we'd put everything inside and locked it, the contents would remain there until we left for the airport. The fridge being lockable meant we didn't have to guard it for the next couple of days, which was incredibly useful. I made notes in my book recording the times that everything had happened during the day, for added security of continuity.

It was then our team's turn to head out for a good meal to celebrate. I'd collected DNA before but never covertly, and I thought what we'd managed to gather was a great success. In the face of a notable challenge too, as the suspect wasn't much for going out, which severely limited our opportunities.

We flew the exhibits back to the UK in a cool bag

and, as arranged, transported them straight to the lab, which kindly had agreed to open early on a Sunday morning to receive the items from us. The fact that we didn't have to store them out of our sight before handing them over was an added bonus in the continuity stakes.

All in all, it was an amazing job. I was pleased with everything we'd accomplished and proud of the team for getting it done so professionally.

It was only marginally disappointing, then, when I received a call a week or so later from the police officer who'd asked us to obtain the DNA in the first place. It transpired that our samples ruled our man out of the investigation – having been considered a prime suspect up until that moment.

I passed on the news to the rest of the team. We'd done a good job in eliminating him from suspicion, because it meant the investigation could now focus on other leads. Sometimes it's as much about ruling somebody out as it is about ruling somebody in, but I knew after all the effort we'd put in it would have been a lot more satisfying had we nailed the guy as the offender.

It was also a slightly bitter pill to swallow as it had been an incredibly costly exercise. However, there was always the chance we could have caught a prolific offender and solved a number of murders. That fact we didn't ensured the investigation kept going after other leads, and that was a positive result for all of us.

As well as the satisfaction the team and I felt about accomplishing what we'd set out to do, I experienced another private feeling of relief. I would never have let on to the rest of the team at the time, but I had no idea if we could rely on the integrity of the local police. I suspected not, but I wasn't about to start asking questions and find out. In countries such as the one we'd visited, many police officers outside the major cities aren't well paid, particularly those on the lowest rung of the ladder. If you're a foreign criminal on the run, one of the first things you do in a new country is to find someone who could alert you to anyone sniffing around your trail, and pay them off.

I know this happens because it's a scenario I've faced once before, and I've experienced similar situations in other countries, where I've had to be mindful not only of those we were in the area to observe, but also of those watching us.

Cambodia is undoubtedly one of the most sorrowful countries I've ever visited, as I've never seen such poverty or such levels of child abuse before. Children there are treated as a commodity, something to be bartered for and exchanged. I found myself there to track and film child abusers who regularly flew out from the UK in pursuit of their prey, and to meet the men who trafficked children. There was no doubt in my mind, early on during our trip, that the local police had been tipped off to our presence. With the possibility of being jailed for infringing the privacy of those we were monitoring, neither myself nor the cameraman was going to argue with the hostile and angry group of security men who stopped and surrounded us.

We didn't know if they were who they appeared to be, or if they were undercover police. They demanded the cameraman show them the footage we'd already shot, and then insisted we wipe the memory card clean of everything we'd filmed. If we didn't comply, they threatened to seize our equipment and destroy it. We were happy to oblige because the camera holds two memory cards, which the operator can switch between. We told them we'd not shot anything and, as the cameraman switched from one card to the other, we showed them the blank. They never knew we kept the material we'd recorded.

For the job in Cambodia, I'd travelled in disguise and under a pseudonym, in order to meet traffickers who told me they would provide me with children. Long before flying out there, I had decided I would need to change my appearance, but I wanted it to look as natural as possible, so I dyed my hair ginger, let it grow, grew a beard and moustache, and wore glasses. I told very few people where I was going.

Once I'd gathered as much information as I could about the Cambodian pimps, including a lot of under-cover filming in some risky situations, I was able to supply the local police with a substantial dossier which, in the months after my return to the UK, led to the arrest and prosecution of a number of offenders. I was a bit wary about handing over this file; I thought there was a possibility that a corrupt police officer might want to arrest me for infringing other people's right to privacy, so I took a couple of precautions beforehand. I made copies of everything; one to take back home, one to pass to local groups. These charities, which are involved in protecting the children and tracking the movements of foreigners who come to the country with the specific purpose of abusing children, are well placed to monitor the situation there, and I'm still in touch with them.

I've also been able to confront men both here in the UK and abroad who have, after grooming them either in person or over the internet, abused or attempted to abuse children. Being able to talk to people, the sort of people routinely referred to in the tabloids as 'monsters', and getting them to put forward their side of the story, is a useful way of gathering more intelligence and enabling convictions where possible.

You have to weigh up the risks, and in some countries I haven't been quite so cavalier. In the UAE, for instance, I chose not to travel with a cameraman. For one particular trip to Dubai, it was just myself and David Wells, my lawyer friend.

David is someone I've known for a long time, over

ten years now. I first met him when he was representing Barry George, who was falsely accused of murdering Jill Dando, and we subsequently became friends. He has always worked in the area of miscarriages of justice – he writes for *Inside Times*, the magazine for prisoners – and he's an incredibly smart guy. He's the complete opposite of the *Rumpole of the Bailey* type of barrister – he's very forward-thinking, and thinks more like an investigator than any other lawyer I've come across. Like me, he's driven by the desire to do what's best for his client, and not by money. His skills complement mine well and together we're a good team.

David and I were in Dubai on an intelligence-gathering operation, so we had no plans to film anyway, but once we arrived and saw the two men we were after, I was glad we'd left the cameras at home. It transpired that the pair – both high on the 'most wanted' list back home in the UK – were pally not only with the local police but also with prominent politicians and sheikhs. Being caught clandestinely filming them would have had serious consequences, so David and I had to be careful to give the impression that we weren't anything other than two holidaymakers having a good time. We returned to the UK and passed on to the police what information we'd gathered; extradition proceedings for the two men are currently under way.

When work takes me abroad, I often don't tell people (apart from my family, of course, and one or two others) until I've returned. It affords me some protection as, to all intents and purposes, people think I'm still in the UK. Say someone thinks they spot me walking past them on the streets of a foreign city and they're not sure if it's me. They might look online and see that my Twitter feed makes no mention of being abroad – hopefully they'll just assume it must have been someone else they spotted.

I'll even go so far as to post things on social media to give the deliberate impression that I'm still in the UK. I don't want to make it easy for anyone to get me into trouble. I've enough experience to know how to deal with most situations on home soil, but it focuses the mind when you're abroad and the challenges are greater.

One such investigation that could've ended badly involved a trip to Turkey. Our intention was to try to film the smugglers who take people into the country from bases in North Africa and then on to beaches on the Greek islands, but it's difficult to get into Turkey as a journalist. We would've tried to get in via the traditional route – applying for visas – but even if we'd been given permission to film, we would've been allocated a government press officer and wouldn't have been able to do our jobs properly.

Instead, we – myself, a cameraman, and a close protection officer for security – simply took a boat in ourselves. When we were stopped, we were identified as journalists and given permission to stay for the rest of the day, but had our equipment confiscated. But not all of it. We'd managed to hide one of the smaller cameras under a pile of jackets and we used that as we travelled around and did what we'd set out to do. Even this was tricky, though, as we were followed everywhere by plainclothes police officers. In hindsight, maybe they were secret police. We didn't stop to ask. We were only allowed to stay for a short while, as the police were hypersensitive to our presence there. We were permitted to observe the beaches for two hours (where we filmed surreptitiously) and then had to leave.

There's always a risk that we can be slung into prison and I have to gauge the level of possibility – what are the chances of the police arresting a high-profile journalist and putting him in jail? They're pretty slim in most countries, but there's always some element of danger there. As I said earlier, I always have to take the lead when we're abroad (after taking David's advice) and give the crew confidence that everything will be OK.

It's always easier back in the UK where I'm fully aware of what I can and can't do under the law, and where I can usually ask someone if we can do something – such as filming on their premises – which then solves any problem if they give us permission. I've found that as long as I explain to people – owners of cafés, restaurants or bars, for example – why we are there, and why we have our cameras, they're usually happy to cooperate.

This happened a number of times when we were filming *On the Run*, which aired on ITV from 2011 to 2013. The concept was to apprehend wanted criminals who'd jumped bail – which we did successfully, catching nine people who then went to jail for a collective thirty years. In one episode, the team and I cornered someone wanted for armed robbery in Swansea, in the Mumbles area. We intended to confront him in a local café so I went ahead and spoke to the owner.

'We're doing this investigation and I'm looking for a guy who's wanted for armed robbery,' I explained. 'He's going to turn up here this afternoon. You mind if I just sit in the back room, behind the till and the bar, and wait for him to turn up?'

There's always the possibility that the owner might say, 'Hang on, I don't want an armed criminal in here. I'm going to close the place early and you can all clear out.' But we can usually reassure them that police officers will be right outside and get involved as soon as we've positively identified the offender. It also helps that I'm a big guy and appear confident in what I'm doing. It gives a certain authority to what I'm about.

That's exactly what happened in this instance. As the guy came into the café and sat down, I strode out from the back and confronted him. He told me unconvincingly that it wasn't him I wanted, it was his cousin, who just happened to be waiting outside. What a coincidence – that's right up there with 'the dog ate my homework', that one. He began to edge towards the door, but just as it seemed he might try to make a run for it, the police steamed in and arrested him.

For all those straightforward confrontations, there were those that didn't go quite as smoothly. On another occasion, we were running surveillance on a firearms offender who was on the run. We received a tip-off that he might be in one of the two different addresses he was known to frequent, so the team and I plotted up in two cars, one outside each house. After a while I got a call from the other vehicle; it seemed someone had taken exception to a man sat in the back seat of a car near their house, doing nothing but staring out the window, and they'd called the police. I had to drive round to explain to the cops who'd turned up that, far from being a burglar looking for opportunities, the suspicious man was my producer and working with me on the right side of the law.

They were pretty good about it, although the information that we were in the area should have been passed on more clearly. Maybe we should have told them exactly which day, and which street – that might have helped. More often than not, the police tend to work with us as they understand what we're trying to achieve. We're pursuing the same end goal, after all – catching the baddies.

It doesn't always go that way, however, and relations with the police on one of the most challenging episodes we filmed were not good. I failed then – and still do now – to understand why, when all we were doing was assisting them in locating and recapturing a dangerous man. Stephen Blake, from the West Midlands, had been on the run for about a year, after he'd been convicted (in his absence) in July 2012 to serve eight years for firearms offences and harassment.

The year before, Blake had threatened a couple he believed were sheltering his girlfriend. He'd made sure that the man, Ben Simmonds, had been round to his home and handled a sawn-off shotgun that Blake kept under a tarpaulin beneath his ferret hutch. As his threats escalated, he told the couple he had 'a tool in a bag' that had 'enuf [sic] DNA on it'.

Blake was convinced that he had no reason to fear a visit from the police, who'd learned about his threats to the couple and his possession of the firearm. He believed that only Simmonds's DNA would be found on the weapon, and his aim was to frame Simmonds as part of his harassment campaign. So convinced was Blake, in fact, that he told the police to go ahead and test the gun. However, forensic analysis revealed that he hadn't been successful in this attempt to cover his tracks. Rather than face the court and the inevitable sentence that would follow if he was found guilty, Blake chose to abscond.

When he eventually turned up in court after we caught him, having being in hiding for a year, his defence barrister claimed he'd fled because his heroin addiction made him think irrationally and he hadn't wanted to miss his daughter's first birthday. Ironically, his love for his daughter was to play a significant role in his recapture.

We started the process of hunting for Blake in the same way we did for anyone who'd gone on the run; we began with the family. Whenever someone disappears, they're going to need to be sustained, wherever they are. By and large, either family or friends help offenders hide and evade the law. We started with Blake's mother, who lived in Redditch – we simply sat in a car outside her house and watched. For several days. Eventually, we thought we caught sight of him leaving the house through the back door, and although we tried to follow him we lost him pretty quickly. It was evident that he was aware of how to avoid surveillance, and it was no easier trailing his mother. She drove a powerful Lexus and we couldn't keep up with her whenever she left the family home, so we had to rethink our plans.

There had been a degree of publicity in the area about Blake. He was a visible character before he absconded, and the fact that nobody came forward to tell the police that he'd been seen around his mother's home was a sign, to us, that he was feared; more than the fact he hadn't been around. Being feared can work against you, though, and so it proved when someone did come forward to speak to us. On condition of anonymity, he told us that no, he didn't like Blake, and that if we wanted to find him we should go and look at this particular address.

We drove over and looked at the premises. The road it was on was midway between Blake's mother's house and her father's house; we thought there was a chance that the grandfather might know where Blake was, too. From the outside it was impossible to tell who was living at the address, but we walked along the street and spoke to a few of the neighbours. You can quickly tell who's going to be helpful in a local community like that; older people tend to keep an eye on what's happening on their road, perhaps because, like parents with young children, they tend to be at home during the day.

One door we knocked on proved especially useful; the occupant of the house said they'd been concerned about all the comings and goings from the house in question, so much so that they'd started keeping a list of all the cars that stopped there. Make, model, licence plate details. The number of vehicles made me think it likely someone in that house was supplying drugs; if that was the case, maybe someone at the property was also sheltering Stephen Blake. I wondered if we should bring in a heat-detecting camera and train it on the loft, because I was sure we'd pick up signs of marijuana being grown in the roof space there. This would give us a reason to talk to the police and get them to raid the place.

There was a simpler alternative, however. We could sit on the address, and watch closely the movements in and out of it. Clearly we couldn't park outside, as we'd be pretty obvious to anyone inside, so we had to bide our time in the car a little further away and come up with a scheme to allow us to see what was going on.

One of our young producers suggested that we lower him into a wheelie-bin, cut a hole out of the side, and put him in the street outside the house so that he could monitor what was going on. I told him that it wouldn't work; it would be too cramped and too cold. 'How about in the car, then?' he persisted. 'I could lie in the back and observe from there?'

That had its merits so I agreed, only he didn't want to get into the back initially, he wanted to drive down the road himself and then climb in. I wasn't sure this was a good idea but he could see no reason why it wouldn't be fine.

He drove down, slipped into the back and sure enough, a little while later I got a call.

'Mark, there are police outside, they want me to come out, what shall I do?'

A resident had seen him clamber into the back of the car and called the police; they were standing outside the car while he urged them to go away. Eventually they agreed to follow us to a local retail park where we could tell them who we were and what we were doing.

It goes to show you, people who don't know about surveillance often think there's nothing to it, but they don't consider all the things that could, and most likely will, happen.

As a result, our surveillance operation on the house was pretty much blown. We decided instead to walk up to the front door and simply ask about Blake. The guy who answered the door knew of him.

'Oh, aye,' he said. 'He was here, but that was ages ago, about ten months back.'

That was frustrating, but at least we knew that he had been there. Although the information we'd been given hadn't been up to date, at least it wasn't deliberately misleading. We informed the police about the possibility of the house being used for the distribution of drugs, and then rethought our approach. We decided our next move would be to observe the grandfather, follow him once he left the house, and see where that led us.

The short answer is, not far. We trailed him in his van one Saturday morning as he went on a circuitous route, which at one point saw him head down a cul-de-sac. Of course, we didn't know it was a dead-end. We only realized when we'd got halfway down the street, keeping what we thought was a reasonable distance, only to find ourselves staring into the grand-father's face once he'd turned around at the end and was driving back. We couldn't risk being seen behind his van again, so it was back to square one.

Still, we thought, the van itself might be an indica-tor of something. It was big enough to be used in moving furniture and other large items. Had Blake moved recently? Had he heard we were in the area, looking for him, and relocated?

I had an idea which I wanted to put to the team. First, though, I had to research it. I rang someone I'd previously had contact with, a specialist who worked in-house for MI5. I explained that I wanted to plant a tracker on a vehicle so that I could follow it while out of sight, and wondered what our legal position was, should we be discovered using it.

'Well,' he said to me, 'using a tracker covertly on a vehicle is potentially an offence, but a civil one rather than criminal. As long as you're careful when placing the tracker on the car. If you damage the car in any way, then that could be considered a criminal offence. Walking on to someone's property to place the tracker would be considered trespass, too, but that's also a civil matter. However, if you can show clearly that you thought the tracker, which is an invasion of priv-acy, was the only way to identify a criminal offence taking place, then you can mitigate the original civil offence. Potentially.'

I felt from what he said that we were on safe ground if we could use the tracker to identify where Stephen Blake was hiding out and then remove it without anyone being any the wiser. I put this to the production team; investigative TV programmes had been trying to work out a way to use trackers legitimately for years, and the team agreed we couldn't have come up with a better case in which to employ one. Based on what we were able to deduce about the extent of the liability, everyone agreed. So we went ahead. Our next move was to come up with a plan to covertly place the tracker on Blake's mother's Lexus.

The device we decided to use was one that could be run from an app on a smartphone or a tablet. It allows you to track the car but also input commands such as a ring fence. Once the tracker leaves the area you've fenced off, the app starts to ping and you can follow the vehicle. This meant we wouldn't be alerted if all Blake's mum did was head down to the local shops. It also saves on battery life. On top of this, the unit would go into 'sleep' mode if the vehicle hadn't moved in a while.

In other cases where I've used a tracking device, I've had to go to a garage that sells the same model of vehicle as we're proposing to use the unit on, so that we can get underneath and try out various spots where it would work – wheel-wells are often best, but in some vehicles, they're made of some sort of polycarbonate, and metal is necessary for the strong magnets in the unit to cling to. In this case, we were far from our home base and a friendly garage owner, so we thought we'd be brazen about it, walk past the car and put the tracker in place as quickly as we could.

We did this at about one in the morning. I made my way around the Lexus with one of my team, then stood back and observed, to make sure no one was watching, while he swiftly stuck the tracker in place. It took no more than twenty seconds and we were away.

Later that morning, at about ten o'clock, we checked on the unit via the app. The car hadn't moved, so we went to grab breakfast. An hour or two later, the app pinged. The tracker showed that the vehicle had left the ring-fenced area and so we rushed to catch up to the moving vehicle, but stayed out of sight. I followed the moving blip on my tablet till it came to a stop. We drove past, and saw Blake's mother hadn't left the car, but was talking to someone outside the vehicle; then she headed back home. And that was it.

The following day, the same thing happened. About mid-morning, the app pinged and we set off in cautious pursuit of the Lexus. This time, however, the car carried on driving out of town. Blake's mother drove quickly but the tracker meant that we could take our time and still know which way it was heading. We carried on in this way until the signal disappeared abruptly.

Completely. We drove back and forth around the area, narrowing down the search zone to a few hundred square yards, but there was no sign of the Lexus.

Two of us jumped out of the car and started walking around, peering up farm tracks, wandering on to forecourts and caravan sites. We had a few ready excuses if we were challenged – our dog was missing; we were looking around to see if the area was right for our elderly parents to move to; we wondered if this was a suitable place for us to build a new house – but no one came out and spoke to us. And there was still no sign of the Lexus.

We rang the tracking company. How could the signal disappear like that?

'Are you near pylons?' the chap on the phone asked. 'They could interfere with the signal.'

I was immensely frustrated; we'd been working on catching this guy for nearly a month now, and had felt like we were getting close, but then the prize had slipped away.

Baffled, we headed to a nearby pub to sit and think over a meal, and hope the blip reappeared. Our electronic devices were slowly losing power so we plugged our phones and tablets in behind a bench of pensioners, who were amused by the amount of tech we had. When there was enough charge on my device, I had a brainwave and looked at the unit's tracking history. Sure enough, although it had gone silent because the car was stationary, there were the same repeating GPS coord-inates. I looked on the map and saw it was a farm.

'I've got it,' I announced to my colleague when he came back from the bar.

A farm in the middle of nowhere – it had to be Blake's hiding place.

I rang the camera team and told them to get to us right away. We met on the road near the entrance to the farm. 'I want to go and take a look now,' I said to my producer. 'I want to be certain he's in the house. And when we call the police to arrest him, I want to make sure he's inside.'

'Be careful,' my producer warned. 'He's a danger-ous man.'

My surveillance guy and I wandered down the lane leading to the farm. It was now late in the evening, so we weren't likely to be spotted, but the excuses we'd had at the ready earlier in the day would sound false if we were challenged now. We hadn't come across this place before because it wasn't signposted on the road, and was hidden behind a long hay barn that ran alongside the lane; we had to go past it to see there was a bungalow there. Around the building were fields filled with crops, making it easy for anyone inside to see people coming and going. By now, it was nearly 11 p.m., and we agreed that we'd try to get as close to the house as we dared, to see if we could actu-ally place Blake inside.

We knew Blake was a big video-game player – his Facebook page contained a number of links to different ones – and when I looked through a window at the side of the house, I caught sight of a large TV with someone in front of it playing a video game. Although I couldn't see enough of that person to be certain it was Blake, it was a good first clue. However, what we saw in the garden was the clincher. There on the lawn was a child's playhouse, the kind made of big plastic panels. Even in the dim light I could see it was bright pink.

It was then that the dogs in the house started barking and we heard movement inside – as if their owners were going to let them out – so we beat a hasty retreat down the lane. I quickly checked the images I'd kept from Blake's Facebook page as reference points, and there was a photograph of his daughter's outdoor playhouse. It was bright pink. Identical to the one on the lawn. We'd got him.

We decided to come back the following morning with the police. I didn't want to take any chances, though, so tasked one of the team with contacting the owners of the rented property, explaining to them who we were and why we were interested in their house, and to ask for their permission to enter the premises.

The following morning we regrouped at the site at 6 a.m. We dropped off one guy by the woods on the far side of the fields. Armed with binoculars, he would keep a close eye on the house to make sure no one left and fled from the road. He was also going to see if he could spot Blake so that we could inform the police that we'd positively identified him and were sitting on the farm to make sure we would have sight on him at all times if he moved.

Sure enough, it wasn't long before Blake was seen at the kitchen window.

'I've seen him,' said my surveillance guy. 'One hundred per cent it's Blake.'

We rang West Mercia Police to tell them we'd found him. It wouldn't be long now before a confrontation could take place and our excitement continued to build. However, a farcical dispute occurred when we revealed his location to the police. It transpired that Blake was on the territory of a different force and a tussle took place on the phones as to which force had jurisdiction and would therefore arrest him.

All in all it took four hours to resolve. No wonder Blake had been able to stay on the run for so long.

My team and I weren't inactive during that time. We kept sight on the house, and also heard back from the owners. They were shocked to learn who'd been renting from them and immediately gave us permission to walk on to the premises and enter the building if that would assist in arresting the offender.

Once the police finally decided who was going to apprehend Blake, we were called and asked to present our evidence at a police station. I thought, 'No, that's not right, why would we leave the site?' So I refused to go, and suggested instead that we meet in the car park of a nearby pub. I went with my producer but left the rest of the team in place on the farm.

The sergeant I spoke to asked to see the intelligence we'd gathered so that she could be brought up to speed with what we knew and why we were so certain it was Stephen Blake on the farm.

I ran through everything and then asked, 'So when are you going to carry out the arrest?'

'Oh, we're raiding the place now,' she said.

I was outraged. 'That's disgraceful. The only reason you know Blake's there is thanks to us. We want to film the raid and you're pulling a trick like that to try to keep us away?'

I started running out of the car park, calling to my producer as I went.

'Ring the team now, get them to follow the police in. I'll be there as fast as I can.'

I ran to the lane so quickly that I managed to get there before the police, so I carried on towards the farm with my team.

Down at the bungalow, at the sight of six men racing up the lane carrying camera equipment and boom mikes, a woman came flying out of the house.

'What do you think you're all doing?' she yelled. 'Clear out of here, you've no right to be here.'

I explained who I was.

'We're here to find Stephen Blake. And we do have a right to be here,' I told her. 'Where's Blake?'

'He's not here,' she said. 'Haven't seen him in months.'

'Well, he is. We've seen him,' I replied.

'He was here, but he left earlier,' she retorted.

'Did he, now?' I asked. 'Because we've had people out back and down the lane, and none of them saw him leave.'

To give her credit, she kept trying. 'Oh, yeah, he saw them, so he left a different way.'

'Which is it, then?' I asked. 'You've never seen him – then he was here – then he vanished mysteriously?'

Waiting for the police to arrive, I heard my phone start pinging again – Blake's mother's car was on the move, no doubt coming here to see what was going on. It was at that point that I heard loud banging from inside the bungalow; lots of it. The woman went back indoors while I rang the chief inspector with whom I'd been dealing prior to that day. I told him what had happened and how the sergeant had tried to do the dirty on us, but that no officers were here.

'Ah,' he said. 'They're meant to be there.'

'Well, they're not. So we'll secure the premises till they arrive.'

Shortly the police vans appeared. They too asked us to leave the site but I explained again that we had the authority of the owners to be there. The female occupant of the house came out again at the sight of the police, and was particularly abusive, but the police ignored her as they went about their search. It wasn't a big place and before long they all trooped out again, saying Blake wasn't there.

'Is there a loft in the building?' I asked.

The officer replied that there was but there was no way Blake was in there as it was tiny. I told him I'd heard a lot of banging before they arrived and that they should check again. Sure enough, a team of officers went back inside and within thirty seconds I heard a shout: 'He's here, we've got him.'

The loft was small but Blake had smashed through the partition that had been boarded up and was hiding in the small space behind it. A great sense of relief that we'd done our job properly went through the whole team as we waited outside.

After a while an officer came out and spoke to me. Blake wouldn't come out while we were right there, he explained, and was threatening to kill himself. We stepped back slightly, and about forty or so minutes later, Blake came down from the loft and was walked out of the house by the police.

I told one of the officers that I was going to have a few words with Blake on camera while the police finished their business inside, and she was happy for me to do so. Blake said the same sort of things people I've caught while they're on the run often say – that they would do it again if they could, just sneak away from court and live freely for as long as possible before someone found them. He'd managed a year.

When Blake finally did go before the judge, charged with harassment and possession of a prohibited fire-arm, all he received was an additional six months on his sentence. Hardly a robust way of dealing with things, in my opinion.

We had one final thing to do before we left the farm. Once Blake's mother arrived, we waited till no one was looking, then removed the tracker from the back of her car. No one was any the wiser, till now.

I'm also working on a case where I hope to make a difference to a long-running police investigation by talking to some people that the police really can't approach for assistance. Drug dealers – particularly the bosses – aren't a group that the police can usually have a casual chat with. Imagine: a police car pulls up outside a house, a couple of officers walk in, they sit with the owner of the house for ten minutes or so, then walk out and get back into their car. What's everyone going to think? That the owner of the house is cooperating with the law? That the police are in the pocket of an organized crime boss? – because the neighbours will know that's who lives there. It doesn't matter which side you stand on; it doesn't look good for either party.

But if you're in my position, it's different. I can go and knock on the door and the men inside will know I'm not a threat to them. I can explain the situation calmly and carefully, and usually they will listen because they know they won't be compromised by talking to me. I can ask for information, without having to offer anything in return, and maybe move the case along a little further.

In this particular case (I can't give specifics for legal reasons), a young woman had gone missing, and so much time had elapsed since her disappearance that the only hope the family had left was that her remains would be found, and that whoever was behind her disappearance – and probable murder – would be brought to justice. The family had offered a reward, but the people most likely to know something about the crime – the people for whom the reward was intended – were exactly those people who would never hear about it. That's why I asked the officers working in the area who the Mr Bigs were, so that I could pass on the information about the reward.

I'm a firm believer that the passage of time has an effect on people's attitudes in relation to a crime such as this. Loyalties shift and change; overheard conversations take on a new significance when pieced together with fresh information that comes to light; people cannot always carry the weight of a secret inside them. There is also the possibility that someone out there has known something for a long time and it can take only one thing to trigger a desire to speak out – and money can be a great driving force in loosening tongues.

The police gave me details on four individuals. These guys are all high up the chain, controlling the city's drug supply. Their stories involve serious money and serious violence to go along with it. I heard stories about drug deals gone wrong, kneecappings, innocent people caught in the crossfire, that sort of thing.

I decided to pay each of these four men a visit – well, three of them; one of them was in jail. Of the remaining three, one individual's wife was particularly abusive and so I never managed to get near the front door, let alone speak to him personally. However, the other two did hear me out.

The first guy lived in a massive house, and it was fortunate that his wife was on her way out as I walked up to their door. The case I was working on was well known around the city, and there was a general desire to see it concluded. When I explained who I was, this individual's wife let me in to speak to her husband. With the other guy, I went round to the back of his house and he was standing there with his dog – both of them were huge.

On both occasions, I explained who I was, what I was doing in their town, and why I'd come to see them. Before I'd even opened my mouth, the big guy said, 'I know who you are,' which was a little unsettling in the circumstances. I was clear that I wasn't there to investigate them in any capacity, and that I was visiting them for one reason, and one reason only, which was to help find the body of the missing young woman.

I let them know about the reward, and that if anybody they were in contact with knew anything, if anyone had a lead that could help the missing woman's family, would they please consider passing it on. I explained that I wasn't asking them to go and do anything criminal, that I simply thought they should know, and that they might know enough people to get that news around. As a result, they might be able to get an answer for us.

The two guys listened, which is all I could have hoped for. I went to see them respectfully and I hoped they took it in that way. Perhaps something will come of it – some little bit of information might get shaken loose. You never know.

I paid these visits alone with no back-up in the car. I did keep my phone turned on, though, with a contact at the other end in case something unexpected developed. I've taken risks like this in the past, but they're always calculated ones: is something likely to happen? Are they going to attack me? Is something going to kick off? How isolated am I? Can I reach for my phone and can I call someone?

If I'm in the UK and about to go somewhere potentially dangerous, I'll make sure to call someone beforehand – usually David Wells – and then keep the line open so that they can hear what's being said and do something should they hear anything unpleasant happen. Other times I might have someone waiting in a car around the corner – they'll have their phone open so they can hear me too.

Although I do push the boundaries somewhat, I'm always conscious about managing my own personal safety and, when I'm working with a TV crew, the safety of the people with me. Even more so, of course, when I'm with a team carrying out some covert filming and we're in potentially dangerous locations. In those situations, I ensure I'm wired up with a mic so that everything can be recorded, and I'll have a small camera fitted to me as well. The footage is never really good enough for broadcast quality, though, so there's usually a camera operator with me too. I'll usually have a quiet chat with him before we go in to wherever it is we're going – a club or a house, or wherever it is. I'll make sure that if he's uncomfortable at any point and wants to get out, then I'm out too – and vice versa.

Speaking to men like the drug dealers wasn't the only thing I did in relation to the missing woman's case. I'm working with a search team, and we've identified spots in the local area where there are likely places for a body to have been dumped. If we can find the young woman's remains, then it will not only help the family, but there might also be vital clues left on the body as to who committed the crime – such as the material the body might have been wrapped in. I have also spoken to a number of people who, over the years, had either not spoken to the police before or whose evidence had never been properly followed up. This evidence included sightings of the woman that corresponded to what the family had supposed had happened to her, and suspicious activity by two men in the vicinity who were known to the victim and her family.

I thought the two men might be able to shed light on what had happened and I went to speak to both of them, but neither one wanted to talk to me – one wouldn't even open his front door and shouted through it instead, telling me to go away. My view in these circumstances is always the same: if you've done nothing wrong, you've got nothing to worry about. So let's chat – give me your side of the story. If, on the other hand, you refuse to talk to me, that suggests that you're either concealing something that you've done or you don't want to be confronted about the past in any way.

What do I think really happened? Elsewhere in this book I've written about the nature of opportunistic crime, about stumbling on a potential victim by chance.

I don't think that's what happened here. I think the young woman was deliberately targeted – for what reason, we're unlikely ever to know. Until such time as the promise of a reward can tempt someone to tell me – or the family, or the police – what occurred, the victim's family will have to carry on suffering.

3

INTERVIEW WITH A KILLER

STEPHEN BLAKE MAY BE IN JAIL, BUT THERE ARE times when even a guilty plea, a conviction and the sight of an offender being taken down to spend the rest of their life behind bars will never ease a family's torment over the death of their loved one, as I saw in south-east London following the death of Tia Sharp.

When I was putting together the documentary for ITV on Tia's case, her mother, Natalie, showed me a photo taken for a prospectus that Tia's school had prepared for incoming pupils at the beginning of the new academic year. The photo showed her daughter carefully using some chemistry apparatus, safety glasses on. She looked every inch the pupil her teachers and friends described to the newspapers: happy, confident, a credit to her school. The tragedy was that Tia posed for the brochure but never got the chance to start the new school year. No new beginning for twelve-year-old Tia; instead, a miserable and sad end at the hands of someone she trusted.

In the summer of 2012, London – and indeed the rest of the UK – was bathed in the optimism of the Olympics. Performances by British athletes at the Games set new standards for the country's sportspeople to aspire to, and the anticipated problems – a terrorist attack; atrocious traffic clogging up the capital's roads; unhappy tourists; public apathy towards a sporting event that ranked several levels below the more popular sports of football, rugby, cricket and tennis – all failed to materialize. It was a time when the country seemed to come together.

On Friday, 3 August in south-east London, however, a child went missing from a deprived housing estate, and the media descended.

Tia Sharp, the nation was told, had left the house where her grandmother lived in New Addington, near Croydon, to go out for the day. She'd not been seen since. Her mother and grandmother, Christine Bicknell, were both distraught.

Tia often stayed at Christine's house and even had her own room there. Also living in the house was Christine's boyfriend, Stuart Hazell. Tia was very fond of Stuart – her grandfather, as she thought of him – and would often spend time in the house alone with him, as Christine's work as a carer meant she sometimes had to stay away from home for the night.

I didn't like Stuart Hazell from the moment I met him. Along with the rest of the media, I'd gone down to the house in New Addington on the evening of Sunday, 5 August to report on Tia's disappearance, on what the police knew or suspected, and on what I could find out about Tia and the family. I'd spoken briefly to Tia's uncle, David, and was able to get a clearer picture of Tia and what the family thought might have happened to her. It was while I was talking to him at the front door that Hazell came into view warily, standing in the hallway to see who I was.

Hazell was a strange-looking bloke, an air of neediness hung about him, and I didn't warm to him, but he didn't make any comment at that stage. I went away and did some research on him. Before he lived with Christine, he'd been in a relationship with Natalie, Tia's mother. He was known in the area, had some minor convictions for small offences and wasn't much liked. I learned that he'd been bullied at school and was considered to be something of a failure. He was, I thought, worth looking into further.

It seemed that not everyone shared my views of Hazell. No police officers were on duty outside the family's front door that evening; there was no sign of anyone watching Hazell's movements, or the movements of anyone else who came in and out of the house. I couldn't understand that. It's well known that when a child goes missing, or is killed, the first place to look is inside the family home – the chances are high that the culprit is someone connected to the relatives.

One common misconception people have about crimes such as abduction and murder is that they are often committed by a stranger. A sound at the window, the banging of a door somewhere in the house, the creak of a tread on the stairs. It's an easy thing to imagine – that, lying in our beds or standing about in our homes, we could be murdered. The truth is, it does happen, but rarely at the hands of a total stranger. What about our children? Every parent knows the dread of thinking their child has wandered away from them in a street, or a shop; and there have been terrible stories about the outcomes of such incidents – James Bulger being one of them. But your child taken from your house, abducted from their own bed by a stranger? It's unlikely, no matter how much we might fear it. In the UK, there's not been a single case of a predatory paedophile entering a house and abducting a child where the occupants are unknown to the offender.

My background as a former family liaison officer meant I understood the process of early stage investigation and how important it was going to be for the police to share information and get the media onside in Tia's case. As an FLO, you're placed with the family to be the point of contact between the investigating team and the family; but you're also there to keep a close eye on them, to see how they behave and to watch for any signs that things aren't as they claim to be. In Tia's case, the family had been assigned an FLO but the police presence was lacking.

Not only were people coming and going from the grandmother's house, seemingly with no one checking on them or their connection to the family, but there was also press all over the place. Not that I can complain about that – my time as a serving police officer was long behind me and I was now a member of the press myself. However, it concerned me that there was little sign of the event being managed by the police, who appeared to me to be stepping back and letting things unfold for themselves. I hoped I was wrong, and that someone was keeping a careful eye on what was going on, but I was far from certain.

That Sunday night we recorded a simple appeal from Tia's uncle David for Tia to come home, which was broadcast on ITV on Monday morning. The following day the crew and I returned to New Addington to broadcast some more reports, and approached the family again. I knew that they would have to talk to someone in the media, and I wanted that person to be me. It's part of my job, to try to get the news first, but I was also learning more and more about the case and I wanted to get inside the house to see what else I could uncover.

By Wednesday, it was pretty clear that Stuart Hazell

had been the last person to see Tia before she vanished. A neighbour of his had told the police that he too had seen Tia at about the same time, supposedly just after lunchtime on Friday the 3rd, walking away from her grandmother's house, but it was Hazell's declaration that was definitive. The more I learned about the case, the more certain I was: Tia was dead and Hazell had killed her. Why, and what he'd done with her body, I didn't know, but I was sure we'd find out.

Tempers on the estate quickly began to run short. It's not uncommon for this to happen; the residents are almost always wary of the press and media coming to neighbourhoods such as theirs in times of crisis, writing about 'sink estates' and how communities are being lost to crime and drugs. It angers those residents who feel it's an unfair depiction of their home, designed to appeal to readers up and down the country in rather better circumstances than their own.

At one point, some irate residents became quite aggressive with the crew and me. They ignored our security guy and started shouting past him, 'Fuck off' and 'Clear out of here.' I tried to reason with them and explain that they needed the media's support and our help to publicize this story to keep it alive. My words seemed to have an effect and they stopped resenting our presence as much, but not fully. We were still intruders in their eyes: here for the headline and then gone.

I spoke to the uncle again, and made it clear that it would be really good to have a word with Stuart Hazell. I explained that I knew Hazell hadn't spoken to the media yet, and maybe he'd like to give me an interview so that people could hear directly from him.

The process of setting up the interview began there. I knew that how I approached Hazell, and what I said to people who would report back to him, would not only help him make his mind up as to whether he gave me an interview but would also – if we did go ahead – make him either relaxed or put him on the defensive. If I went in demanding to speak to him, saying things like 'I know he's got more to tell us', that would only put his back up. I didn't want that. I needed him to see me as something of a confidant, someone he could open up to, someone he could relax with when talking to.

During my time in the police service I learned how to put a suspect at ease, if required, as it's often the best way to get information out of them. Sometimes you have to go the other way – you have to back them into a corner, pressure them, provoke them even – but in most cases, behaving as if you're in step with them will get you further.

Tia's uncle phoned me that night.

'Mark, can you get here straight away?' he asked.

I explained that I lived some distance away and that I wouldn't be able to get a camera crew there quickly.

He told me he understood. 'Stuart wants to do an

interview. He's spoken to the police today but he's happy to talk and he'll talk to you. What time can you get here in the morning?' I told him I could be there by 6 a.m.

As agreed, I was outside the house early the following day but no one emerged. I spent the next few hours phoning David, waiting and drinking coffee. Eventually, he rang and told me that Stuart would be ready to start some time soon. By then it was nearly midday. Initially, I'd planned to get the interview in time to broadcast on *GMTV*, but we'd gone way past our slot. So I spoke to the editor of the lunchtime and evening news programmes.

My pitch was simple: 'We need to get this story on the main news today because there's a really big story here. I'm convinced Stuart Hazell killed Tia Sharp.'

Down the line I could hear the editor pull the phone closer. 'How'd you know that?'

'It's just a feeling at the moment,' I said. 'OK, I know that sounds slight, but there's nobody else in the frame. He was the last person to see her alive, nobody else has any input that would suggest otherwise.'

I went on to spell out how odd I thought it was that there seemed to be no one from the police watching him.

'It appears they're not following him as a line of enquiry, which could mean they're trying to get him to think he's not a suspect while they've got surveillance stuff inside the house, listening to him. I don't know if that's the case, but they certainly aren't keeping a watch outside the house, which is strange.'

This was a guess, of course, but keeping an eye on Hazell using covert surveillance was the only thing that made sense to me, given the absence of an officer outside the home.

'What do you want to do?' the editor asked.

'Let's do a double-camera interview. That way I can keep one on him the whole time rather than have to do cutaways afterwards. If I'm right, he won't want to do this more than once.'

If we had only one camera, we'd have to keep it trained on Hazell and then reshoot my questions a second time, hoping he would hang around long enough to be in the frame as we filmed. This is standard practice in TV interviews. However, using two cameras would mean we wouldn't have to bother with that, and we wouldn't need to film my reaction shots after the interview. The editor agreed and two cameramen soon turned up with their kit. We went to sit in the ITV broadcast truck that was parked around the corner from the house, not too far away.

The crew and I talked about how I wanted to run the interview. I explained that right from the moment they started setting up, whatever happened, they shouldn't stop running the cameras. They should keep recording all the time.

'If Hazell says something off camera to somebody, I want to catch it – he might give something away when he thinks he's not being filmed.'

I made my suspicions clear to them. 'This is an interview with a killer, there's no doubt about it.'

About half past two, maybe three o'clock that afternoon, a journalist from one of the newspapers came to the truck door. 'There's someone looking for you, Mark,' he said.

David had come out of the house and was calling out for me. He'd inadvertently set off a scrum of journalists and photographers, all of whom wanted to get their own scoop. I rushed out and ushered the uncle back inside. 'Let's get indoors,' I encouraged him.

I didn't want the media looking over my shoulder and I didn't want Hazell to come out and speak to us where everyone could overhear and where I couldn't ask him everything I needed. I wanted a proper interview with him.

I asked the crew to wait outside the house while I went inside to meet Hazell. He and I sat down and he asked if I'd give him the questions ahead of the interview. I told him that wouldn't be the case and explained why not.

'Any other journalist would have a set list of questions they'd want to put to you. They'd want you to answer the questions they ask – it's about them and their agenda. I don't have one, I want to hear from you. It's important the interview flows, so I'm just going to ask you some very simple things to start you off. The questions won't be difficult, and if you can't answer them, then you can't answer them. Don't be worried, I'm not trying to trip you up.'

I maintained an open, friendly manner when talking to him, as non-threatening as I could manage. I didn't want to give any indication that I believed he was involved in any way – even though I was convinced of his guilt.

While the crew came in and busied themselves setting up the cameras and sound equipment, Hazell and I went into the kitchen. Outside, through the drawn blinds, we could see and hear the massed ranks of the media outside. I thought I'd test the waters and see how he replied to the most obvious of questions.

'Where do you think Tia is?'

'Some fucking nonce has got her, hasn't he?' he replied.

I was a bit surprised he'd come out with this and wished I'd got him on camera already.

'What makes you say that?'

'They have, I know it.'

He was quite emotional but said nothing more, so I told him to get himself a glass of water, as interviewees tend to get a dry throat on camera – probably a nervous reaction to the pressure.

The crew called out that they were ready so we made

our way back into the other room and started the interview.

Hazell took his seat next to Tia's uncle David on the low settee. Both of them wore specially printed white T-shirts emblazoned with a photograph of Tia below the word 'MISSING'. Hazell looked warily at me as we started talking, as if he expected me to switch abruptly to being aggressive once the cameras were on, but I began by asking him to talk about Tia and her life, which was easy for him to do.

'Did she have any problems that might have caused her to go missing?'

'She's got no problems at all. She's a happy-go-lucky golden angel, d'you know what I mean? She's perfect, no arguments, no nothing. Nothing we could think of, absolutely nothing.'

Talking to me, compared with talking to the police, allowed him to feel that he was being treated as an innocent man, and that he could really let go and open up. And he did. Once he relaxed, I asked him to tell me about her disappearance. He claimed he'd seen her leave the house, but after that, where she went next, 'I don't know.' He also said 'she was seen' walking down the pathway between their house and the neighbour's. Later, it transpired that the neighbour had lied, and the neighbour ended up in jail, too.

Some commentators, watching the interview later on, said that the interview showed Hazell was lying – that his facial expressions demonstrated his attempt to cover up what he'd done. The idea that you can clearly tell whether a person's lying by their body language – the way they move their mouth, how they hold their hands, how they look at you – I don't put any stock in that. Hindsight's a great thing, it has to be said. If there's a foolproof way of knowing whether someone's telling you a lie, I've yet to find it.

There's no doubt that Hazell is a particularly accomplished liar. There are good liars out there, and how I know they're lying, how I find them out, is not from reading 'tells' so much as by listening carefully to them, to what they want to say to me. You have to listen, repeat their words back to them, go over the detail again and again, each time teasing out more information from them – or more opportunities for them to embellish their words or make up stuff.

Paying attention is particularly important, and I weigh up what I hear with the evidence I've already looked at and considered. Some people can be telling me absolutely, totally convincingly, that they had nothing to do with whatever it is I'm asking about, but I'll still consider their words carefully. If it doesn't ring true, I'll say, 'OK, but that doesn't stack up with the evidence.'

You can tell so much from the details that they give you. How do they know that? Could anybody else know that? What's unique about what they're telling me, that's specific to this interview? Why are they telling me in so much detail? Why are they remembering that fact? Are they leaving stuff out? All of these questions are especially important.

During the course of the interview, Hazell started to give away an incredible amount of detail about Tia, specifically how she left the house, what she looked like when she did, the conversation they had. However, the interview was broken up prematurely when Christine, Hazell's partner and Tia's grandmother, came running into the house in tears. She'd been ambushed by the journalists outside when she got out of her car. At what was already an incredibly stressful time for her, the questions shouted at her and the cameras thrust in her face had clearly proved too much. Stuart left the room to console her.

When he returned, I pressed him gently on what he thought people imagined had happened to Tia. What would he say to those people who thought he might have something to do with her disappearance – *did* he do anything?

'No, I bloody didn't. 'Scuse my language, but no, I didn't. I'd never think of that. I loved her. She's like me own daughter, for God's sake. We had that sort of relationship, that sort of thing. She wanted it, she got it.'

I tried to prompt him as little as possible. A TV interview isn't great to watch if the interviewee is mostly silent, so I had to keep Hazell talking, but my aim was to allow him to speak as freely as possible. It's all too easy when conducting an interview to arrive with a list of questions to which you want answers, but this can mean the viewers end up hearing the interviewer's voice more than the person they're supposed to be hearing from.

I knew Hazell had a lot to tell me, and knew that if I could keep him talking he would say something that would likely trip him up down the line. Either in what he'd already said, or in what he would say to the police in the future.

At the end of the interview, Hazell made a direct plea, asking Tia to come home, or to let them know where she was at least, or for any information on her whereabouts. The footage ended up being shown around the world, and has featured on many true crime shows since then, because it's not often you get exactly what I knew it was going to be – an interview with a killer.

When I left the house that afternoon, the media circus descended upon me, demanding to know what had been going on inside, what had been said, what I had learned. Although these journalists and reporters were my rivals, many of them were also my friends and I couldn't ignore them all. This interview was a scoop, though. I'd worked to get it, and I didn't want to give too much away, so if I could avoid answering direct questions, then I would. I also wanted to sort out my thoughts as quickly as possible, as there was a lot to get done to have the interview ready for the news broadcasts at 6 p.m. and 10 p.m.

I explained to the other journalists that I'd done an interview with Hazell for the six o'clock news, that he'd explained to me what he knew and had made an appeal for Tia's safe return. That was it. I went back to the ITN production truck and ran through the interview footage to see what we were sending to London, before feeding down the line the key parts of the interview to ITN's offices as quickly as we could, just like sending an email, so that the files could be cut ready for the evening news broadcasts.

I also needed to shake off Stuart Hazell's thoughts and personality before I set off home, and I needed some peace and quiet to be able to do that. I hadn't liked Hazell when I first met him, and knowing what he'd done made me feel sure it wouldn't be long before he was found out by the police. I knew that he'd killed Tia. I was absolutely certain he'd killed her. Where her body was at that point and how he'd done it, I didn't yet know, but he was the last person to see her. Everything started and finished with him, so it had to be him.

As soon as I could, I got into my car and drove off, but stopped at a service station around the corner, where I parked up for about fifteen minutes. In my mind I ran through what Hazell had said to me, but also what else I could recall about the inside of the house. When I was first in the house on Monday, I had asked the family if they minded me looking upstairs in Tia's bedroom. Tia's mum had said no and I respected that, even though I'm an incredibly nosy person. I didn't ask again. However, sitting there in the car, I wished I'd been able to take the camera upstairs after speaking to Hazell. What was her bedroom like? The police would have searched it, but to have shots of the room after Hazell had spoken would have made even more of an impact – by making Tia feel more real to the viewers – with the interview.

This might sound callous, given we're talking about a murder victim, but that is the dual aspect of my working life; on the one hand, I'm an investigator, seeking out the truth, and on the other, I'm a journalist, whose role consists of putting together an engaging and accurate story for mass consumption.

I finished my journey home and watched the first airing of the interview on the six o'clock news. I was pleased with how it came across and I got plenty of positive feedback from the ITN offices – about the interview itself and the sort of responses from fellow journalists they were getting from its screening. When the programme was over, I went upstairs and called Tia's uncle David, to see if Tia's family had watched it and what they thought of it.

He picked up right away. He thought it was a good interview and then added, 'Hang on, Stuart wants a word.' He must have held the phone away from his ear as I then heard Hazell's voice, calling from across the room: 'Thanks, Mark, really good.' David came back on the line, said a few words and hung up.

'Bloody hell,' I thought. What did he think had just happened? Did he not see what he'd done?

Later that evening, I also watched the 10 p.m. news broadcast, when they used an extended cut of the interview. This time I saw it more dispassionately. I could tell what the viewing public would think: Hazell had to be involved in some way. I also knew that the investigating team looking into Tia's disappearance would all be watching; the police had contacted ITN after the 6 p.m. broadcast to ask for a copy of our rushes. As is the custom, ITN's lawyer phoned me up to check it was OK. I agreed, and though they'd have to go through the process of a written submission, I had no objection to sharing our material with them. Knowing that they were already interested in the footage made one thing clear to me: this interview was going to form the basis of a criminal investigation.

The following day was Friday, and I had the day off to take the kids up to London to see the musical *Billy Elliot*. We'd just got off the tube and were walking up the station steps when my phone went mad. Text messages, voicemails. I skipped the voicemails and started to read the messages. I couldn't believe it: Stuart Hazell had gone on the run and the police had found Tia Sharp's body in the loft of his house. Earlier that morning, before I'd set off from home with my family, I'd tried to get hold of David, the uncle, but hadn't been successful. I'd left him a couple of messages but he hadn't come back to me. Now I knew why.

I called a fellow journalist and friend, the crime correspondent at the BBC, and asked what had happened. He told me the police had searched the house again that morning and had found Tia's body wrapped up in the loft.

'You're joking.'

I was absolutely appalled. I knew the police had searched that loft three or four times that week and hadn't found her body on any occasion – how could Tia possibly be up there? Throughout that whole interview, all the times Hazell had spoken about wishing he could confront the people who thought he was involved, he must have been thinking about Tia's body, upstairs in the attic, wrapped up but slowly decomposing. The summer temperatures would have been hastening that process, and sooner or later the smell of death would have started to permeate the house. Would he have noticed it and wondered when anyone else was going to? Was that what prompted him to run?

My BBC friend went on to tell me Hazell had fled the house, and that the police didn't know where he was. My immediate fear was that Hazell might kill himself. If he committed suicide, then no one would ever get any answers and there would be no proper justice for the family. 'You'd better not do that,' I thought. There are times when a family won't get any kind of truth about what happened, because the offender won't speak, but sometimes they do. Even being able to piece some of the bits together helps.

At that stage I was also disappointed with the police. In fact, I was incredibly angry. How could they let him get away? Why wasn't anybody on the address, watching the premises? Why did they let him go out that morning, bearing in mind that my interview had aired the night before, making it obvious he was implicated in her death in some way? I sat in the theatre with my kids that afternoon, totally distracted and unable to enjoy the show. I fumed all the way through.

Thankfully, later that day Hazell walked into a shop not too far from New Addington. The shop-keeper was alert enough to notice that he was wanted by the police – during the course of the day there'd been quite a lot of publicity – and informed them of his whereabouts. Hazell was swiftly arrested and charged with Tia's murder.

There were two significant repercussions for me. Firstly, a lot of people suggested that I'd been asked to interview Hazell by the police, which obviously would have been a bad idea, given I work as an independent journalist, and something I'd never agree to. Secondly, the rest of Tia's family – her mother, Natalie, and in particular Christine, her grandmother – came in for a lot of criticism. Because of the relationship I'd built up with the family (and the interview I'd done with Hazell), the two women turned to me to assist them in trying to get the truth out – that they'd been duped by Hazell. As a result, I agreed to make a programme for ITV about Tia's death, the investigation, and the subsequent trial and conviction of Hazell, and became quite close to the two women.

I'd been accused of making programmes to assist the police in the past. I'd also been accused of being an undercover officer, still operating for them under the guise of being an investigative reporter. I've even been accused of working for the security services, for MI5, which is absurd.

I'm very supportive of the police. After all, I was an officer for many years. I want them to succeed in their job of catching the bad guys, and I'll do what I can to assist them in that when making my programmes. However, I will not act for them, and I will not carry out interviews for them. If they want to know something that I know, they'll have to watch the TV broadcast like everyone else.

I did have a run-in with the police the year before, 2011, after being openly critical of them during the Joanna Yeates investigation.

Joanna, a landscape architect in her mid-twenties, lived in Bristol and went missing on 17 December 2010. Her boyfriend had been away for the weekend and returned home to an empty flat. Joanna's coat, mobile phone, keys and purse were all in the flat, but their cat hadn't been fed. On Christmas Day, her body was found three miles away, in the snow near a golf course. She'd been strangled.

Five days later, her landlord, Christopher Jeffries, was taken in for questioning by the police. After two days, he was released, but his ordeal had only just begun. He was perfect fodder for the tabloid news-papers, who went to town on him, running various appalling headlines that tore into his character and his past, all without any justification whatsoever.

On 20 January, the police arrested and charged forty-year-old Vincent Tabak, Yeates's next-door neighbour. Tabak had attempted to divert the police's attention towards Jeffries but the police officer interviewing Tabak became suspicious of the questions Tabak was asking him – specifically relating to the forensics the police were pursuing – and Tabak was arrested.

DNA evidence and fibres from his coat linked Tabak to Yeates's body. After initially claiming he was being framed by corrupt officials, when confronted by the evidence (including videos he'd watched on his computer of women being choked) at his trial in October 2011 he pleaded guilty to manslaughter but not murder. He was, however, found guilty of her murder and sentenced to life in prison, with a minimum term of twenty years.

My criticism of the police's conduct in this case began even before the arrest of Christopher Jeffries. I'd driven down to Bristol to report on the case for ITN, and was disappointed to see what I regarded as basic steps being ignored during the investigation. Even the initial response seemed to be giving out mixed signals. In the days before the discovery of Joanna's body, Avon and Somerset Constabulary were telling people not to be too concerned, saying there was no evidence of anything having happened to her at that stage. At the same time, they were advising female students in Bristol to be careful in the winter evenings and not to go out unaccompanied. It was clear that something *had* happened to Joanna.

I was certain that Jeffries had nothing to do with it. His mannerisms, the way he was behaving, all suggested he was innocent; and his whereabouts immediately before and after Yeates's disappearance didn't put him in the frame. I did think that somebody in the locality – perhaps even in the street where Yeates lived – knew a lot more than they were telling the police, but I knew it couldn't be Jeffries. The police told the public and the media that they'd interviewed all the neighbours and had ruled them out. There were people in the vicinity who *hadn't* been ruled out, though, as is evidenced by the fact Vincent Tabak was eventually convicted of the crime.

I filed another piece for ITN after the discovery of Joanna's body, and reported on what the offender had done and what he might be like. I made it clear that I believed him to be local, known to Yeates, and a lone operator.

I made that last point because I'd been told there were marks on the back of the victim's body. Joanna was found immediately on the other side of a stone wall, and I believed this meant she'd been lifted from a car, put on top of the wall, and the offender had climbed over to then lift her body down. This would explain the marks on her back and suggest that he hadn't received any help from a second offender.

I'd also discovered that the area where Yeates's body had been found was still covered in detritus after she'd been removed – sweet wrappers, cigarette butts, all kinds of rubbish that could potentially have been significant. This was a murder inquiry and it concerned me that forensics hadn't taken everything away from the scene. It didn't all need to go off for examination but it should have been secured.

Given the lax way the search around Yeates's home was conducted – and this was before Tabak had been arrested – I wasn't convinced the investigation was being led as sharply as it could have been.

All these concerns made it into my TV report. I was

also a bit critical of the Avon and Somerset Constabulary's press office, which would shut down in the
evenings. In cash-strapped times and under normal
circumstances, this might be considered acceptable, but
not when there's a major murder investigation under
way, with representatives present from the national and
international press.

I spoke to some local journalists who explained that
the chief constable was particularly distrustful of the
press following some negative articles published in
the local papers. It turned out my ITN report was the
last straw for his team. The police banned ITN from
attending their press conferences, and criticized us for
'unfair, naive and irresponsible reporting'. Ahead of
our broadcast report we'd asked them for their input,
which they'd refused to provide, and I felt what we
had said was entirely justified – before this over-the-
top response. Banning us was a strange thing to do,
not least because the other news teams covering the
press conferences simply pooled their footage to share
with us, so nothing was gained from the ban.

The police said they were going to make a complaint to Ofcom, but nothing happened in the end. I
know we made a good report for ITN and I'm glad it
was broadcast; I'm convinced we did the right thing.
If the police get things wrong, I don't worry about
being the one to point this out.

To return to the investigation into Tia Sharp's

murder, the fact that her body remained undiscovered for so long, and following several searches of the house, showed how badly wrong the police got things. How could they not have found her in the loft, which we were told they'd searched four times? When they did finally discover her body, all someone did was reach inside a hatch – she was that close to the edge. And how could they have allowed Stuart Hazell to move about unmonitored, making it so easy for him to flee the house once he felt the net tightening around him? Lucky for them that Hazell is not especially bright. If he were, he might have got a lot further away than the twelve miles or so he travelled to Morden, where he was caught.

After Hazell was charged, all sorts of rubbish started being broadcast about the case. Sky News said that Tia's body must have been in the house next door and moved through the loft, which is utter nonsense. Tia's grandmother, Christine, was initially arrested as well, which led to idiots thinking, 'Conspiracy!' when it was clearly Hazell acting on his own. She was completely innocent, duped by Hazell as much as everyone else had been. Only one other person eventually faced trial: the next-door neighbour, who'd corroborated Hazell's claim to have seen Tia walking away from the house, was later convicted of wasting police time.

There's no doubt that one of the reasons Christine was vilified over those few days was because of who she was, rather than what she had or hadn't done. If you've ever any doubts about the existence of the class system in Britain today, just take a look at the different way we treat the families of victims in a case such as this. Many people judged Christine because of how she looked, where she lived, how she spoke. They didn't take the time and trouble to listen to what she had to say. Christine had nothing to do with Tia's murder, but her arrest led to her being tarred with the same brush as Hazell. If I had been a police officer conducting the investigation I would certainly have interviewed her, but I would have stopped short of arresting her. Being accused of the murder of your own grandchild is always going to be a difficult thing to get over – I imagine it would stay with you for ever.

There were many other things I didn't like about the investigation. I felt it was conducted incredibly badly, and saying it was incompetent would be sugar-coating it. The head of the Metropolitan Police later apologized for the force's failure to locate Tia's body sooner and said they'd investigate why this 'human error [and the] processes and management decisions . . . that led to that failure' occurred.

I worked with Natalie and Christine on the programme – *Living with a Killer* – we'd have ready to air once Hazell was convicted. The centrepiece would be the interview I'd done with Hazell but the focus would be on the two women and what they could tell us about Tia's life. They had no idea how to respond to the huge media attention the case had attracted and its focus on them, and, getting to know them quite well, I like to think I was helpful in looking after them through some of those difficult weeks.

By the time the trial came around, we'd made a lot of the programme – what remained would be some coverage of the trial, the expected conviction of Hazell, and Natalie and Christine's reaction to his sentence.

Hazell's trial was held at the Old Bailey, in Court Two, which is in the old courthouse; major trials take place in either Court One or Two. The room has all the grandeur and atmosphere you'd expect of such an important setting; and to anyone who watched the TV series *Rumpole of the Bailey*, it hasn't really changed. The old wooden dock stands high, the only hint at modernization being the glass surrounding it. Everything else is particularly old-fashioned, with the judge presiding on the huge wooden bench at the front.

As I was covering the trial as part of the programme we were making, I planned on being at the Old Bailey for the duration. The production team also took Tia's family in to central London and back home every day. We did this not just because we were working with them, but because we wanted to look after them too. It was useful for us to bond with them, while it provided some support for both Natalie and Christine and an outlet for them to share their feelings about the day's proceedings.

On my way in to the court on the first day of the trial, I was stopped by one of the police officers who'd worked on the investigation and who had been there when Hazell was taken into custody. He wanted to tell me that the interview I'd carried out with Hazell before he went on the run had been absolutely crucial for the police – they'd studied it closely and found it immensely helpful. He confirmed the prosecution would be using it as evidence during the trial. 'Good,' I thought. 'Very good.'

Sure enough, the prosecution's opening statement involved them playing my interview with Hazell. It gave me a chance to look at the recording in a different light – not as a journalist or a detective, but as an outsider. It showed clearly how the police could and did use it to secure evidence against Hazell. What he said and the lies he told could be challenged by the prosecution.

If you think of it from a legal point of view, rather than a journalistic one, having the opportunity to carry out an interview – a proper sit-down interview if possible, but certainly one where the interviewee is focused on answering your questions – can prove invaluable when you're conducting an investigation, particularly a live one. In the Soham murders case, when two ten-year-old girls, Holly Wells and Jessica

Chapman, were killed by school caretaker Ian Huntley in August 2002, it was Huntley's TV interviews that gave him away. He provided a number of statements to the media over the two-week period between the girls' disappearance and the discovery of their bodies. Scrutinizing the interview footage gave detectives a clear indication of Huntley's guilt.

The police can't task the press to go and conduct those interviews – and nor should they – but when they do take place, the police should be aware of their value. They should stand back and realize they could be especially useful to them. In the past, police forces didn't want those interviews to happen, and such an attitude fails to acknowledge the significant impact a media interview can have, not only in raising awareness of a child's disappearance, but also in catching the killer, particularly if the interviewee has something to do with that disappearance.

It's been seen in other press conferences, such as that of the Philpotts. Mick and Mairead Philpott were convicted of the manslaughter of six of their children in a house fire in Derby in May 2012, and it was Mick Philpott's bizarre behaviour at the press conference that alerted detectives to the pair's possible guilt. If a suspect's story is put into the public domain, it can be properly tested and checked against known facts, and discrepancies can be challenged by those who have evidence to the contrary.

I will never know whether that was the case in Tia Sharp's murder – whether Stuart Hazell was a clear suspect for the police from day one, or from the moment I started speaking to him and he became a suspect to me. I have to say, I don't think it was the case. If it was, why weren't the police watching him in any capacity? Why did they allow him to walk out the door and go on the run?

The prosecution's case continued, and the evidence that came out was shocking. Not only because of its nature, but because of the way in which it was shown. Graphic images were exhibited; during their investigations, the police had found a mobile phone containing a memory card which held videos of Tia Sharp sleeping as well as sexualized photographs of her. Then there were crime scene images of Tia's body wrapped up in black bin bags, and pictures of where she'd been found in the loft. It transpired that Hazell had also been searching for teen porn images on his phone, and it was obvious he had harboured a sexual interest in Tia.

The family, and many in the public gallery, all saw the photographic evidence being exhibited on the TVs in the courtroom. It was incredibly distressing, especially for the family. I wrote to the Director of Public Prosecutions immediately and told him I was disgusted that people in the court other than members of the jury could see these images. He responded and the

TVs in the court were moved so they couldn't be seen from the public gallery at all.

The trial was scheduled to run for approximately four weeks, which is about average for a major case such as this. Hazell, in the box, listened to the evidence and, like everyone else in the courtroom, could see that the case against him was pretty compelling.

Every morning and every afternoon I'd drive in and out of central London with Natalie and Christine, and saw how exhausting the whole experience was for them. The first week drew to a close and we all had a break over the weekend before gathering again the following Monday for the start of the second week. As I sat down in the courtroom that morning, the police officer who'd spoken to me on the first day of the trial came up to me again. He explained that there'd been some movement downstairs earlier in the day, and that they believed Hazell was going to change his plea to guilty.

Well, that was a pretty important development, and not just for the outcome of the trial. The jury would be dismissed and the court would adjourn for the rest of the day to prepare for closing remarks by both the prosecution and the defence prior to the judge's summing up and sentencing. For Natalie and Christine, it would mean that they wouldn't have to sit through any more awful revelations. For me, it meant that our programme would have to be ready to go out within the next day or so.

I left the court quickly and frantically dialled my editor's number. I explained what I'd just heard and how we needed to conduct an interview with the family that day. We knew that the programme would be about Tia and her family – her life and what had been taken away from Natalie and Christine – and we had a great deal of material available to us, not only that with Hazell, but also footage of the case as it developed. However, it needed a beginning and an end.

You might wonder why we hadn't done an interview with the family beforehand. Because the case was a criminal investigation, it was important not to do any TV or radio interviews until the court case had finished. It's always been held to be important in our judicial system that court cases such as this one are heard without prejudice – particularly if any members of the family are planning to give evidence, because they might be considered to be trying to influence the outcome of the case, or be influenced themselves by something they've said or read that others don't know.

The point at which our production team were free to carry out an interview with the family was the moment the court released all the witnesses. Once Hazell had pleaded guilty and this happened, the crew and I quickly took Natalie and Christine to a hotel, conducted an interview in some detail, and started to edit the programme. We were almost there. One more thing had to happen: the judge had to issue his sentence.

Hazell received thirty-eight years, which by any stretch of the imagination is a phenomenal length of time. Without knowing the details of his offence, and in light of the average sentence for murder being around fifteen to twenty years, you might think it was pretty remarkable, given that he'd killed one person. However, the barbarity and totality of his offence was off the scale; he is a really nasty, nasty piece of work.

The real gravity of what Hazell did to Tia is horrific. We don't know exactly what happened in her last hours – he still hasn't fully admitted what he did – but it's clear that immediately prior to her death he started to sexually assault her. She would have resisted fiercely, and I suspect that struggle resulted in a particularly violent sexual assault on her. She then died, and I wouldn't be surprised if the sexual assault continued after her death. Having killed her, Hazell then wrapped up Tia's body and put her in the loft, in a pretty amateur way.

He must have been jumping up to the ceiling when the police came, went through the house and didn't find her. 'How can they be so stupid?' he must have thought. He made no effort to move her body, however. He probably didn't realize this, but because he wasn't even being watched, he could have done so at this stage. He must have known that he couldn't wait too long – as she lay hidden in the loft, the material he'd used to wrap her body in would only contain the smell of decay for a certain period. After a while that smell was going to seep through the house. He clearly had no idea what to do when that did happen.

Tia's case highlights many interesting angles to the investigative process. It's first and foremost a desperately sad case, but it's also one where the media played a crucial role. My personal part was important in terms of both securing the initial interview and the way that interview was conducted. Allowing Hazell to talk without it becoming *my* interview, making it clear to him that it was his time to talk, meant he had to fill the space with his own thoughts – and since all he could think about was lying and lying and lying, this was never going to be a satisfactory tactic for him.

It was also a particularly important case in terms of the way the police operate. It taught me that we're quick to presume that the police have done something you'd consider elementary, but we should never work on the assumption that they've asked that one question, interviewed that one particular witness, or followed a certain line of enquiry. Far too often when we make such an assumption, the reality is that thing hasn't been done. The only way to make sure it's done is to do it yourself.

The case gave me other assurances in my work as an investigator. I had a gut feeling about Hazell from the moment I met him, and I knew that if I got to the family before all the other journalists did, and persuaded them to talk to me, I would be able to get in and probably find out something. I believe it was my interview with Hazell that caused him to panic, go on the run and subsequently be apprehended.

Tia's is a case in which I'm particularly proud to have been involved. I still think about her. I think about the life she came from, and how far down the list of priorities that often makes someone like her. She was a young girl who had a great future: she was driven, she was pretty intelligent, she worked hard at school, and while she was brought into the world in a challenging environment, great possibilities lay ahead of her.

Something I've learned to always ask myself is: have you asked everyone you can think of for their opinion, for their experience? This stems from the aftermath of the Jimmy Savile case, when the Dame Janet Smith Review was conducted. I spoke to one of the reviewing panel – an eminent figure who'd been asked to take part in the review but who had little experience in child abuse investigations, or even doing that particular type of review. However, he had some sort of honour, a 'sir' or a series of letters after his name, I can't remember which.

I remember him replying to my question – had they spoken to everyone they could think of? – with, 'No, we don't think they've got anything to say.' Whenever

I hear those words, it makes me angry. *My* response is that you don't know if someone's got something to say until you ask them – until then you've no idea what information they could offer you. *How* do you know they haven't got something to say? How do you know until you ask them the right question? They won't say *anything* of use until you ask them.

A successful interview is all about the questions asked. There are a lot of people out there who either deliberately ignore anything put to them, or respond with a question of their own – which is often in more detail than the question asked in the first place. In the past, what I've said to people such as the man on the reviewing panel is: if you don't ask the right question, you won't get the right answer. You might not ask the right question until you've asked every single question you can think of.

If you think someone won't tell you anything, or doesn't have anything to say, that's great. Go and see them anyway – if you're right, then at least you've eliminated them from your enquiries. By not asking – and this happens so often – and by failing to ask those questions, you've left a gap in your investigation or in your review. And you have no idea how small, or how large, that gap might be.

Failing to ask the right questions is less of a problem than not asking any questions at all, but there's a knack to interviewing. The key point, as I've stressed and as was shown clearly with Hazell, is less about the questions and more about giving your subject time to respond. Let them speak, listen carefully, and then go back and tease more out of them. Get a bit more detail at every stage.

It may be that your subject recalls someone saying something, and you respond by saying, 'Right, so what did they say? How did they look? What else was going on around you when they spoke to you?' Keeping on at the little details means the interviewee has the chance to expand their story a little bit more. That's because the thing people do – when they're not accomplished liars or are inexperienced at being interviewed – is fill the gap. It's possible to see this all the time when watching interviews on news programmes or vox pops in the street, for instance.

If you have to interview somebody – a suspect – and you want them to give you answers, don't make it easy for them. Ask them an open question – not one that requires a simple yes/no answer, but a proper answer – and then just leave them to talk. Embrace the silence. Let them respond.

Also, as I've already said, when interviewing people it's particularly important for them to feel comfortable talking to you. If I'm interviewing someone, I'll chat about other things first – I'll try to put people at ease. With Hazell, I kept him away from the scene of the interview to begin with so that he could relax with me before the cameras and microphones came out. I needed him calm with me, and tense in front of the crew – those opposing states of mind would force him to look at me as someone 'on his side' and maybe prompt him to say something that he wouldn't have said if I'd appeared as his inquisitor right from the start.

The way you ask a particular question might well elicit more information. Initial interviews need to be exploratory, always inquisitive rather than accusing. 'Oh, so I don't really understand what happened here. Tell me about this, in your own words, explain that . . .' It's a lot easier to get someone to reply to an open-ended question if they think they're helping you.

Journalists often make this kind of mistake by going straight in with the accusation. They have a column to fill, a deadline to meet, and no time to dance around the subject. I, on the other hand, like to unravel the information, let the subject fall over themselves explaining their take on it to me, go back over and over the points to tease out more information each time, let them dig themselves a hole – and then nail them.

There's a case I'm working on at the moment, where I've yet to have the opportunity to speak to any suspects. The murder at the heart of it was a particularly horrific one to read about. Most of what I've been able to do so far involves speaking to a potential witness and reading the case files. However, I know that putting some direct questions to the persons involved in the crime would produce a result, because there are some strange elements to the case – not least of which are two potential miscarriages of justice. There are some significant hurdles to overcome, though: the case is particularly old, and it took place in a foreign country.

4

MURDER IN THE
FOREST

TEN-YEAR-OLD URSULA HERRMANN WAS PROBABLY
much like all girls of her age – ordinary in the sense
that she was happy, carefree and well loved. Her home
was in an area of Germany called Landsberg, in
Bavaria, to the south of the country – about half an
hour's drive west of Munich and not too far from the
Austrian border. It's an attractive part of the country,
full of lakes, forests and mountains. Lake Ammersee,
on which Ursula's home town of Eching is nestled, is
so large that in the summer months paddle steamers
shuttle between the towns on the water's edge.

Ursula's uncle and aunt lived in the nearby town of
Schondorf, less than one mile away, and after her
occasional visits to them she would cycle home along
the lake shore on her red bicycle, following paths
through the woods known as the Weingarten, which
lay between the two towns.

On 15 September 1981, Ursula was on her way back home from visiting her cousin after a gymnastics class, at about half past seven in the evening. She never made it; somewhere along the route, she disappeared. A ransom note made up of words cut out of a number of newspapers was delivered to the family a few days after she vanished. Tape recordings, with the kidnapper silent as music was played, were relayed down the phone to Ursula's frantic parents. A telegram urging them to continue trying to gather the ransom was also received.

Nearly three decades later, German police deduced that Ursula was abducted by a man who lived in the same village, Werner Mazurek. He had planned the kidnapping, the police said, and prepared a hideaway for the child. His plan was to lock her away until the ransom he'd claimed was paid.

He had, according to the police, dug a hole in the middle of the Weingarten, 800 metres from where her bike was later found, and made a box there for Ursula. It was just deep enough for her to sit down in, but she wouldn't have been able to move about or stand properly. Some pink fabric covered one side of the box – for what reason we don't know. Mazurek put in a bucket for her to use as a toilet, and left her a few comics, some cowboy and Indian novels, a radio, some water, biscuits and sweets. A small electric light (powered by a car battery placed outside the box) gave some illumination, and when Ursula was forced inside her prison, a tracksuit, still in its plastic wrapping, had been placed on her lap. Her kidnapper had fashioned some air holes and run a series of plastic drainage pipes up to the ground so that, even though the box was secured and fully hidden underground, Ursula would still have a supply of air.

Except that somehow the air was insufficient, whether because the ventilation pipes became blocked by leaves and muck or – more likely – because the method used was inadequate in allowing the exchange of air necessary to keep Ursula alive. The kidnapper should have attached a small fan, powered by the car battery, to the pipes to ensure enough air circulated around the box, but he didn't. Within a few short hours of being imprisoned, Ursula died.

What happened to Ursula Herrmann on that evening is not clear. The pathologist put forward the view that Ursula was rendered unconscious with the aid of nitrous oxide and then carried to and placed inside the box without a struggle; this theory was accepted by the trial judge as fact. The pathologist reached this view based on finding that the toxicology was negative (although they were unable to test for nitrous oxide) and that Ursula had a cerebral oedema, leading to the conclusion that such an omission meant that she must have been rendered unconscious by nitrous oxide.

It is true that nitrous oxide slows down both the body and the brain's responses, and this would explain why there was no evidence of a violent struggle in the box. However, I am not at all convinced by this opinion. In fact I would challenge these views; where, for example, was nitrous oxide obtained from in 1981? How was it administered to Ursula? At what point was it administered?

What is certain is that Ursula was murdered, and in the moments before her death would most likely have been petrified, and at some stage struggled, and if she had still been conscious when inside the box, which I believe she was, she would have done all she possibly could have in an attempt to be heard by anyone walking in the dense woodland. The torment she faced in her last hours – alone, in the dark – is barely imaginable. One has to hope that her death was reasonably swift, but, as experts have guessed that it occurred any time between thirty minutes and five hours from her incarceration, it's unlikely that it was.

The underground box with its grisly contents was found nearly three weeks later, on 4 October.

That Ursula died on the first night of her abduction, while her kidnapper went ahead with his claims for a ransom several times over the coming days, makes the crime all the more shocking. The kidnapper stopped asking for a ransom only when Frau Herrmann demanded proof that her daughter was alive. As the box, when it was eventually discovered, showed no signs of having been returned to once Ursula had been left there, there is no reason to believe that the kidnapper ever came back to the forest to check on his captive's welfare. Perhaps he did, and found that she'd died; but no attempt to contact the family was ever made again.

This appalling crime became one of the most notorious unsolved murder cases in Germany. Some people have likened it to the Madeleine McCann case, in the way the media and public alike were gripped by the portrait of an innocent young girl meeting such a foul end, and with no indication from the police that they were ever going to be able find those responsible.

However, twenty-nine years later, in 2010, following the discovery of a tape recorder in his possession that was exactly the same type as had been used to make the ransom demands, police arrested and charged Mazurek with the crime. He was found guilty and sentenced to life in jail. No doubt Ursula's family was delighted that the man behind such a vile, evil plot – who had smiled and waved as he passed the family home for a year before he moved away – was now locked up for the rest of his days.

Except the family is not delighted. Not one bit.

No one could accuse the police of reacting impetuously and arresting just anyone who fitted the kidnapper's profile – it had taken them nearly three decades to get to this stage. Offenders are hardly ever convicted and jailed such a long time after a crime has been committed. For the victim's family to be so disappointed by the result happens even more rarely. What is it that has made Ursula's family doubt the conviction of Werner Mazurek?

I received the initial message from them through my Facebook page one Thursday morning in July 2018. Michael Herrmann introduced himself, explained that he'd seen the television series I'd made, *The Investigator*, and wanted to talk to me about the death of his sister. I got back to him via Skype, as he'd suggested, and we spoke at length. He told me that he was Ursula's brother and, because the crime isn't widely known outside Germany, he gave me a detailed account of what happened to his sister all those years ago. He also told me what the family thought had really happened, because, according to him, Werner Mazurek had been wrongly convicted.

Michael also made it clear that the family believed that the kidnapper – the killer – had got away with it, scot free. Now that the police had someone behind bars, the investigation had effectively come to an end. The death of his sister was still in every moment of his life, just as it was for his parents – the thought of her horrible dark and lonely end. He couldn't rest until he knew that the right person – or people, because he was certain that it took more than one person to carry out the construction of the box and the abduction of his sister – had been identified, caught and sentenced.

The police were sympathetic towards Michael, and had involved him in their investigations over the years. Although they continued to talk to him about the case, he felt sure they'd stopped thinking about anything other than Mazurek's guilt. Why wouldn't they? A successful conviction for a long-standing, traumatic case would be a big win for any police force, and when the case was as high profile as this, then it was even more likely the police would figuratively down tools, thinking they'd got their man.

Michael Herrmann thought a different approach was required and decided to contact me. 'There isn't anyone here in Germany doing what you do,' he told me.

Certainly in Europe I'm quite unique in what I do. There are investigators in the US working in a similar capacity, but no one on this side of the pond, as far as I am aware. Working on cases that originate abroad is more complicated, though. Often I won't have heard of the case, which can be a plus but usually means I'm unaware of the context (similar crimes, media expectation and pressures on the police – that sort of thing). From a logistics point of view, they're always going to be more complicated. I'll have next to no relationship with the police, I'll usually need a translator and I won't know the necessary protocols for requesting files and other information – all of which makes me more of a hindrance in an investigation than an asset.

Fortunately, in the Ursula Herrmann case, Michael spoke good English, and I had little difficulty in understanding him, which was just as well, as I don't speak much German. He explained that he was working with a friend of the family who was able to translate not only anything sent to me but also any documents from the police files that I might wish to see; he had a good relationship with the police and even though they believe they've caught the right guy, they've been willing to provide him with copies of their investigation files. The family friend, Barbara Zipser, was based here in the UK – she too had written to me on my Facebook page, along with Michael. Dr Zipser is a lecturer in History at Royal Holloway, University of London, and she specializes in linguistic analysis of Greek medical texts. She has provided the family with a lot of support but her willingness to translate everything for me would make a massive difference.

Once I'd agreed to take a look at the case, and after some preliminary reading to get up to speed, my first thought was the obvious: what is the basis of Michael's objection to the conviction? Why doesn't he believe the police's case?

Michael explained that he had many questions about his sister's death, but mostly they stemmed from the same point: how could the accused have accomplished this alone? Werner Mazurek's wife had been charged alongside him, although she was then acquitted at the trial. She didn't seem like a credible accomplice, though – not if it meant she had helped to carry the materials into the forest to construct the box inside the hole (a hole which would have been difficult for one person to dig) and then forced a no doubt unwilling victim into the box. There was no physical evidence of any sort linking her to the crime. Not only that, but the evidence against Mazurek seemed (to Michael) to be pretty weak. It was mostly based on the fact that the accused was in possession of the same type of tape recorder as was supposedly used by the killer when he tried to extort money from Ursula's family all those years ago. The device was a fairly standard tape recorder – the expert witness from the state police came to the conclusion that it was 'likely' that it was used in the crime because the one found in Mazurek's office in 2005 had a technical defect that would have explained why part of the jingle that had been played over the phone was slightly distorted (one tone was not as loud as you might expect it to be).

I know how police think – at least here in the UK – but I doubt there's much difference between the way the German and British authorities look at things. There's a long-standing, unsolved crime, and it hinged upon a few vital elements. If someone from the area, already known to the police, turns out to have the exact same sort of recorder that was used by the perpetrator – well, the chances of that happening purely by coincidence in such a small town are remote. Simply having the recorder was enough to convince many of the police working on the case of Mazurek's guilt. If it was enough for them, it should be enough for the court – and so it had proved.

It wasn't enough for Michael, though, nor was it enough for me. He was right. Nobody could have done all of this – conceived the crime; dug the pit in the middle of nowhere; built the box; filled it with the battery-powered light, the bucket, the comics, food and drink; stalked the girl as she entered the woods; taken her by surprise from her bicycle and tied her up (perhaps?) or knocked her out (maybe?); carried her to the remote spot in the forest where she was somehow lowered (struggling? compliantly?) into what was going to become her coffin; devised and sent demands for a ransom for her safe return using different techniques (a ransom note, telephone calls, even a telegram) – all on his own. More than that, a confession from a man who claimed to have dug the hole in the forest on behalf of Werner Mazurek – something else the police thought proved his guilt – was shown to be false and based on press reports rather than on actual physical knowledge of the site.

Michael explained that these elements of the case caused him to doubt the guilt of Werner Mazurek, and that, in his opinion, the wrong man was in jail. He also had another card to play. Actually, more than a card – a bomb that destroys the case against Mazurek completely.

There had been another murder. Many years later. It bore no relation to Ursula Herrmann's killing, although it took place a mere twenty-five miles or so away, in central Munich. The victim was a fifty-nine-year-old woman, Charlotte Böhringer, beaten to death in her own flat on 15 May 2006. Her nephew, Michael told me, had been convicted of the crime, but her family – his family – didn't believe he was guilty of her murder. I listened patiently to Michael as he gave me the details.

Apparently, there were shoe prints all over Charlotte's apartment that could not be attributed to Benedikt Toth, the nephew. Charlotte's friend Marianna had been round earlier in the day and Charlotte had told her she was expecting a visitor – Marianna thought she'd said her lawyer, but he denied this. After drinking one glass of wine, Marianna left. The bottle of wine was found, later, emptied. The killer had struck Charlotte and killed her with his right hand; Benedikt was left-handed.

Then came the bombshell.

There was DNA evidence in the apartment, Michael

told me. Samples had been taken from a glass in Charlotte's dishwasher and from her dressing table. The DNA had been analysed and neither Charlotte nor Benedikt could be linked to it. What's more, the DNA was shown definitively to have come from a male rather than a female suspect – and the system had thrown up a match. The DNA found in Charlotte Böhringer's apartment in 2006 was identical to that found on a screw that had been part of the box in which Ursula Herrmann had died. The DNA matched neither Werner Mazurek nor Benedikt Toth, nor anyone related to them.

Separated by distance and time, and with seemingly no other associating factors, the DNA is inescapable evidence of a connection between the two cases. It took me only a second to realize the implications of all of this.

'It's impossible to picture how these two crimes could be linked,' I said to Michael, 'so we have to address the issue of cross-contamination. Was the laboratory that tested these samples keeping strict protocols? Is there any evidence to show they had contaminated samples in previous cases? What's the likelihood that two samples would be contaminated by the same earlier DNA? If we have no satisfactory answers to these questions, then there are some further implications, none of them particularly good for the German police. If it's correct that there is a link, then two men are now in jail for two killings that can be linked by DNA samples that demonstrably come from neither of them, so both are – or at least one of them is – innocent. If either of them acted as an accomplice to the person who left the DNA sample, why was only one person's DNA found at the crime scenes – and not either of theirs? To me it's inconceivable. How else can this be explained?'

There's not much hope that Ursula's case will be reopened at this stage, according to Michael. After all, the police won't want to do so – you don't review a case if you've caught the offender. German police forces are generally competent but in one respect they're the same as any police force in the world – they will, on occasions, make mistakes.

Police forces in the UK are considered more accountable these days with police commissioners, who can scrutinize the conduct of investigations and it's now enshrined in police process that after a major investigation is launched, reviews will be conducted at regular intervals to ensure that no one outcome is being pursued at the expense of others just as valuable, because of an investigator's own experiences and expectations. However, there can still be problems with the outcome of an investigation – look at Barry George. He went to jail, but he clearly didn't kill Jill Dando (see Chapter 10).

When I was a detective and investigating the

disappearance of schoolgirl Ruth Wilson from Dorking in November 1995, I carried out a review on other outstanding missing persons cases, including a longstanding case that was on Surrey Police's books for decades. A young boy, Roy Tutill, was brutally raped and murdered in 1968. He was only fourteen years old. I reviewed the case files to see if anything jumped out, but it didn't. It'd been reviewed by different officers at regular intervals over the years – that's how determined the force was in trying to catch the offender.

The attack on the boy was a particularly cruel one. He was then strangled with his own school tie. Roy's body was eventually dumped outside the gates of a large house belonging to the Beaverbrook family, not far from where he had been abducted.

Eventually – over thirty years later and quite by chance – the killer was caught. Brian Field had been convicted of crimes involving young boys previously but was, by the turn of the millennium, living as invisibly as he could in the West Midlands. In 1999 he had been caught drink-driving after leaving a pub and had, as part of that case, been required to submit a DNA sample. In the intervening years, methods of DNA recovery from crime scenes had improved and, fortunately, Surrey Police had retained and preserved Tutill's trousers in a freezer. A DNA sample had been retrieved from them when those recovery techniques improved, and Field's sample, when entered on to the database, threw up a perfect match. Shortly after being arrested and confronted with the DNA evidence, Field made a full confession.

There have been other instances of items from historic crime scenes yielding DNA to modern techniques, which have allowed police forces to trace and convict offenders who must have thought they'd got away with their offences. The Scottish serial killer Angus Sinclair (see Chapter 9) was identified after forensics officers decided to hang on to items in the vague hope that forensic techniques would improve in the future. Fortunately for them, and not for Sinclair, that proved to be the case.

Bearing all these things in mind, I told Michael I'd look into his sister's case, and at the same time asked him to email and post me as much material as he could.

Meanwhile, Dr Barbara Zipser was quoted in an article about the case in the *Sunday Times* on 30 September 2018. The paper reported that she had analysed the initial ransom note – the one made up of words cut out from several newspapers – and, with the aid of linguistic profiling techniques, deduced that the author of the note was 'well educated'. She added that the sender suffered from 'a thought disorder' at the time they constructed the note, and may have been on drugs as well. The *Sunday Times* reporter said Dr Zipser's work 'prompted a flurry of German media attention' and gave more fuel to the campaign to re-examine the conviction of Werner Mazurek.

Once I started looking through the files myself, it didn't take me long to spot a glaring flaw in the police's approach to the case.

Among them were transcripts of interviews that the police had conducted with two pupils from the school in Schondorf located next to the woods where Ursula Herrmann was abducted. Landheim Schondorf is an elite boarding school attended mainly by aristocrats, and admitting international pupils as well as German students. At the time it offered places to students between the ages of ten and nineteen, with about 250 pupils on roll, many of whom had experienced difficulties at their previous school. Today, the school offers special tuition for students unable to meet the academic requirements to sit exams at a state school.

At the time of Ursula's disappearance, the school ran compulsory crafts classes in the afternoon, including carpentry and joinery. A visitor to the forest found a treehouse that some of the pupils at the school had built deep in the woods. Under the ground, at the base of the tree, was a large stash of empty beer bottles. The pupils used to use – and still do now – the forest as a playground; whereas other children in the area tend to pass along the paths by the lake shore and are not as familiar with the smaller footpaths and clearings. Michael told me that the forest, which belongs to a wealthy family, had been less well managed back when his sister went missing and was more overgrown than it is today. In the area where Ursula's body was found in the box, the forest cover was particularly thick.

The police had visited the school as part of the investigation back in the 1980s, and two boys – by then in their late teens, so they'd be in their fifties now – came forward to speak to the police about something they'd found in the woods.

The two students claimed to have discovered a length of wire in the forest, linked to Ursula Herrmann's imprisonment. They'd removed it and taken it back to school, according to them, and then kept it till one day one of them decided to measure it with the aid of a girlfriend. The girl stood at one end of the school running track, holding the end of the wire, while the boy unspooled the rest of it so as to be sure how much he held. When the police came to the school to talk about Ursula Herrmann, the two boys decided they should tell the police what they had found.

I read the account that the two boys gave to the police. One of them named the girlfriend, who was English. It was explained that she 'was on a school exchange, she is originally from London, and at present she is in Paris'.* So I flipped through the papers,

---

* All quotes here are taken from the police files, translated by Dr Barbara Zipser.

but could find nothing more about her. I couldn't believe it; the police had been told by one of these two boys that a third person had been present when they held evidence related to Ursula's abduction and death and they – the police – had made no effort to contact her. They hadn't asked the local police where she lived to interview her and they hadn't made any effort to travel to interview her themselves. In other words, they hadn't taken any steps to corroborate the testimony of someone who – at the very least – had specific knowledge of one aspect of the crime scene.

This was definitely an avenue worth pursuing in my own investigation. If this woman hadn't been interviewed before, she might have something to say that was well worth hearing. Even if she had nothing to say that helped the case, in speaking to me she would rule out some unanswered questions. Why had no one even bothered to approach her?

I started to look more closely at the testimony given by these two ex-pupils to the police. Michael had included their interviews in the files he'd sent me because, I learned now, he wanted me to consider whether or not they were more likely suspects than Werner Mazurek.

The police file starts with an explanation of why they were interviewing the two boys. Two years after Ursula's death, the police had visited the school. During this visit, the police spoke to pupils individually who were at the school when Ursula was abducted. On 18 January 1983, the day after the interviews were conducted, the two boys handed in to the police 'a board with the green bell wire wrapped around it'. They explained that they'd found the wire a year before in the Weingarten, along the shoreline near a hut in the woods. The wire, they told the policemen, ran for a distance of over eighty metres, strung from tree to tree. They'd taken it, wrapped it around a fallen tree branch, and brought it back to the school. They did this, they said, because they couldn't understand why the wire was there.

When one of the pupils and his girlfriend went to the school running track to measure the wire, he then rewound it on to a board that he had constructed especially. Then the other boy put the board into a box, and locked it, where he said it was kept until they handed it over to the police.

As part of the school's curriculum, each pupil at Landheim Schondorf has to undertake a project involving their own research. The project of one of those two students interviewed by the police in 1983 involved studies along the shoreline of the lake, within the boundaries of the forest.

In the subsequent interview recorded by the police, this student explained that he and his friend had found the wire by chance as they were chasing an owl through the wood one afternoon, following it down the hill towards the lake, during the course of the study. According to him, the wire ran from near the hut, either hanging from or wrapped around the trunks of the fir trees. It didn't appear to be attached to anything at either end and was 800 metres from where the box had been discovered.

The wire was bell wire – was it some kind of signalling device? Although the police put no assumption to the two boys in the interview, the suggestion is that the wire was some part of an alarm system for Ursula in her box. For her either to be able to make contact from underground or for the kidnapper(s) to know if someone came near. Or perhaps it was intended for a lookout to use. Maybe it was intended as such, but it certainly seems that it was never connected. So the chances are that although it was set up in the woods as part of the kidnap, it was never properly employed.

The interview with the two boys continued and the pair make a couple of noteworthy statements. The first relates to their reason for handing in the wire in the first place: 'Because we are unsure, whether it was possible for this wire to be connected to the crime, we decided to make our case known to the police. We handed the wire over to the police voluntarily and are happy for the police to use it at any time for potential further investigations.'

It is dangerous to rely on translations as evidence of something worthy of investigation, even by someone with Dr Zipser's impeccable credentials, but this is surely odd. Did the boys think the wire was connected to the crime and therefore they should hand it in, or did they worry that the police already believed the wire to be connected to the crime and so they concocted a story for why they had it and why it was covered with their fingerprints? Either interpretation is plausible.

As it turned out, the police *were* aware of the wire, even though it seems they hadn't connected it to Ursula Herrmann's death at the time. When the fire brigade attended the site to assist with the search for and, later, removal of Ursula's body, the fire officers said they had seen the wire but they didn't move it. Now, without any photographs of the wire in place, it's hard to know exactly how it was supposed to work, if at all. Was it something the kidnappers had planned to install but were interrupted midway through their work?

Michael Herrmann certainly thinks the latter is possible. He told me that he thought perhaps the boys wanted to know whether the police had noticed the wire, realized it was important and had then left it at the crime scene as a trap, to see who would collect it and take it away.

Secondly, one of the boys stated to the police that the wire has been kept securely for the past twelve months: 'Until I handed it in to the police, I had locked it up in a box with a lock on it. This box is in my room, and only I have a key to it.' Barbara Zipser says that the German word for 'locked up' – *'einsperren'* (the boy uses the past tense in his testimony, *'eingesperrt'*) – used in the interview can only be applied when describing the locking-up of people, and not objects, not even metaphorically. Again, we have to be wary about placing too much emphasis on words such as this – after all it is possible it could be a transcription error by the police – but it is an odd choice of phrase.

With more assistance from Michael and Barbara, I started to look into the two boys' story further.

I considered the nature of the crime itself. I thought it was obvious that it would have taken more than one person to carry out – not just digging the hole, constructing the box, buying and fitting it out with the comics and food found inside it, and doing all this in a public space so having to have a reason to be going back and forth into the woods regularly, but also in dealing with whoever they abducted and imprisoned.

I didn't think it wasn't professionally done either. Now this might seem like a funny thing to say in relation to a crime, particularly one with such a horrific outcome, but I mean that whoever carried it out showed limited knowledge and little foresight as to how the crime was going to end.

For instance, what did whoever kidnapped Ursula

envisage was going to happen if their ransom was paid? Were they always going to let the girl die, or would they have let her go? The efforts they'd made to ensure that she was safe – albeit for a limited time and in a limited way – suggested that they expected her to survive for a few days at least. Did they think they could open up the box, lift her out and let her walk free? If they were inexperienced, did they naively think that threatening her would be enough to keep her quiet?

Not having a clear idea of how their plot was going to end is a sure sign of the kidnappers being individuals with limited ability to consider the ramifications of their actions. It calls to mind the case of Shannon Matthews in the UK. Nine-year-old Shannon was hidden by her own mother, Karen, who, with the aid of Michael Donovan, the uncle of Karen's boyfriend, claimed her daughter had been abducted, with the aim of collecting a reward when she was eventually released. Fortunately, Shannon was found alive and well, but it's hard to believe that her mother really thought that 'releasing' the child at a local market, then telling the police she'd been set free by the kidnappers – which would allow Donovan to claim the reward and split it with Matthews – was going to work. It shows a limited understanding of how complex the situation would become when outside agencies became involved, and I think that same limited comprehension of events is on show in Ursula's case.

However, some aspects of Ursula's kidnapping demonstrate a degree of intelligence, and this is backed up by Dr Zipser's review of the ransom note, which suggests it was the work of someone well educated. Someone well educated, but with a limited understanding of how the world works – which to me suggests someone young.

If I'm right – if Michael Herrmann is right – and these two boys (or men, as they are now) have questions to answer, then oddly I don't think Ursula Herrmann was the target. I don't think they planned on who to kidnap and ransom – Ursula simply happened to be the unlucky girl who came along. Maybe they – whoever 'they' were – noticed that some children cycled or walked alone through the woods between Schondorf and Eching, or perhaps Ursula was the only one.

If someone was going to target a child to abduct and hold to ransom, I would have expected them to have chosen one from a wealthier family. I think it much more likely that the two or more kidnappers made their plans, built their box, then took the first person who came past on the day they decided to act. They probably didn't even know who Ursula was until they grabbed her, which is another aspect of the crime that marks it down in my mind as amateur – an adult would have seen all the ways in which that kind of approach could go wrong.

I wonder how the moment of the kidnap occurred. Once the family had alerted the police to Ursula's disappearance, her bike was found fairly quickly, only twenty-four metres from the path where she was abducted. No attempts had been made to conceal it. Had Ursula been stopped under some pretext, grabbed, somehow subdued, bound and gagged? She wasn't tied up when her body was found and during the post-mortem no sign of physical trauma, such as you'd expect from a blow to the head or similar, was found.

This leads to another point that Michael made to me. He believes, and I think he's right in this, that the kidnappers didn't know that Ursula died so soon after being put into the box. As soon as she'd been declared missing, police started to comb the Weingarten. With so many officers at work in the forest, the kidnappers wouldn't have wanted to risk going back to check on their captive in case they were caught. The ransom demand must have gone ahead without the kidnappers knowing Ursula had died within hours of her imprisonment. After all, they thought she'd be OK for a while as they'd provided everything she needed for a couple of days – food, water, air. Not anticipating that they wouldn't be able to visit Ursula again, with so many police in the area, is yet another demonstration of the kidnappers' inexperience.

Which maybe explains again the wire found in the woods. Was it meant to be connected to something that would have allowed Ursula to contact them?

There are so many unanswered questions about the case – the way it was planned; the way whoever carried it out went about choosing the site, digging the hole, carrying in unobserved the wood and tools necessary to construct the box and building the box; the choice of victim; the way Ursula was abducted and forced down into the ground.

For me, there are two aspects to it: one is the planning involved in constructing the box, the other is the choice of victim. It was clearly a planned crime – although I think Ursula was a girl who happened to cross the kidnappers' path at the wrong moment. I can't see how she would have been pre-selected. I'm sure she was chosen at random and that she was there on a day the offenders wanted to snatch someone.

The fact is that most crimes are opportunistic. A window is left open at the back of a house; a handbag is left unattended on a table in a café; a fight breaks out at a railway station after a football match. Similarly, most murders are opportunistic. Domestic killings aside – those where a family member kills someone else in the family – murders committed by a stranger are usually the result of someone stumbling into a situation that fits the killer's needs and desires.

A serial killer such as Peter Tobin (see Chapter 9)

might prowl an area that he thinks will likely yield a victim of the type he prefers, but he won't have chosen that specific victim in advance. A paedophile might chance upon a child on a road and snatch her, driving off quickly and leaving no one any the wiser as to who, why and what happened. The very nature of a stranger murder being opportunistic means events sometimes occur that cannot be anticipated or analysed.

It's what makes those types of crime especially difficult to police. That particular beauty spot, that particular road, that particular moment when two people who have nothing in common cross each other's path in a place neither knew they'd be in advance – it's not easy to cover every single eventuality and follow every possible bit of evidence, because in situations like that, the permutations are practically infinite.

When murders are planned, however, it's a lot easier to trace and catch the offender. In today's world, following someone in order to plan an attack will leave a trace – whether in the physical world through CCTV, or online, where tracing someone's digital footprint, such as their browser's search history, will show what research has been done. The ubiquity of mobile phones now means it's straightforward for the police to trace individuals as they move around an area: calls are logged and positions can be triangulated to reveal someone's whereabouts. Social media is a dead giveaway too, revealing connections between people – in a lot of murder cases, the murderers give themselves away.

No police officer likes the mystery of an opportunistic murder. The myriad elements that put an offender into a position to commit such a crime mean there is often no logical explanation to assist the investigation, and no immediate resources are available to trawl through. The crime has simply happened. In a few cases, investigative officers go to great lengths looking into a specific person, only to find out that the evidence uncovered completely rules them out of any involvement in the offence. In some ways that's a good result, but nevertheless it's somewhat frustrating for the team that has spent a great deal of effort obtaining that evidence in the first place, only to be left with the key question still unanswered.

In Germany, children start school at the age of six and leave at either sixteen or nineteen. Young people can get a driving licence from the age of eighteen. Schools usually run compulsory first-aid training classes at the age of fifteen, but new drivers are required to complete another first-aid course for the driving licence at the age of eighteen. Perhaps having that knowledge recently planted in their brains made the young men think they were capable of placing a girl into a sealed box and keeping her 'safe' in the ground.

I've now spoken to the girlfriend. She knew nothing of the case and she definitely doesn't recall measuring the length of the wire on the school running track. In fact, she doesn't remember a wire ever being mentioned. She has clear memories of her time at the school, and is certain in her recollections. She also says that she found one of the boys – not her boyfriend, the other one – a little frightening, and not just because he kept a handgun at the school.

I've now traced these two men, who I consider persons of interest; one of them still lives in the area, the other resides elsewhere. I'd like them to provide a sample of their DNA voluntarily, so it can be tested against the samples held from both Ursula's and Charlotte Böhringer's murders. If they decline – but why would they, if it ruled them out of committing crimes of which they are totally innocent? – then I would have to take further steps.

There are other people whose DNA we should check against the samples – other members of Charlotte Böhringer's family – because the more people we can rule out, the closer we get to finding out what actually happened to her. Which might help with Ursula Herrmann's case.

Why would those boys lie about the wire? I'd start my questions by asking them to tell me again about the discovery of the wire, and what they subsequently did with it. If their story is a fabrication – if what they told the police *is* a lie, designed to explain why their fingerprints were all over an item close to the site where Ursula was hidden – then even after all this time, maybe there is something to be uncovered.

5

MY CRAFT: THE FORENSICS OF DEATH

ALTHOUGH I LEARNED MUCH OF WHAT I DO FROM MY time in the police, approaching drug barons for their assistance didn't feature in any training manual. However, like many things in life, you don't learn everything you need to know in a classroom. So many of the skills I put to use in my day-to-day duties as a police officer were learned on the job; and although I've taken all those skills with me into what I do now, I've also learned so much more since becoming an investigator.

There are things I miss about being a police officer – being able to arrest offenders being the main one – and there are things I don't. Working for the police meant dealing with the fringe element that appears after major crimes such as murders. I've had to handle 'input' from mediums and clairvoyants, and also from the fantasists who admit to crimes they haven't committed.

It's certainly one of the downsides of policing; you

want publicity for a case, because publicity means more witnesses come forward, and more people will be your eyes and ears, but publicity can work two ways. An individual who confesses to a crime – but only once the media appeal has been launched – can be the type of person who craves attention, who needs some sort of recognition. You'd think it would be obvious if someone approached the police and said they'd committed a crime when they hadn't, that they were suffering from a recognizable mental illness, but it's not always so. And sometimes people, offering what they think they saw or heard, genuinely think they're helping – when they're not.

There are also the deliberate time wasters. In the case of the disappearance of one young woman, a man living two hundred miles away from the city from which she'd disappeared came forward to accuse a local man as the murderer. It was pretty clear to the investigating officers who travelled down to interview him that he held some sort of personal grudge against the man he'd accused, but his chief motivation was the prospect of a free lift to that city (arranged so that he could attend a line-up).

It almost goes without saying that something I had to learn on the job, and which has sadly only become a greater part of my work since I started my current role, is an understanding of the processes of death. It's just one of the many grim things I have to know how to handle that most people probably don't want to think about.

I've been present at many post-mortems, and I'm no longer upset when watching one. However, the first time is quite shocking. The pathologist starts with a careful examination of the naked body from the outside, looking for identifying marks such as tattoos as well as for evidence of trauma or any medical indicators, such as needle marks or recent scarring. This is the point at which bruising or any other markers of blunt force will become evident.

When it comes to the internal organs, they are removed in three blocks. First, the throat, tongue, heart and lungs; second, the liver, stomach and minor organs; and third, the kidneys, intestines, bladder and reproductive organs. Each organ within the block will be examined carefully, weighed and then, if necessary, dissected for tissue and fluid analysis. The brain is removed once the pathologist has used a small, hand-held saw to cut open the top of the skull. Again, the primary examination will be a visual one. If something such as a brain haemorrhage has occurred, this will be immediately obvious. If there is nothing to see, samples for microscopic analysis will be prepared.

Observing the aftermath of death in the clinical, pristine environment of a laboratory or its equivalent is one thing. It's a different matter altogether when you're required to look at corpses found in the open, or concealed somewhere. That requires a deeper understanding of what happens to the human body in the days, weeks, months – and even years – after someone dies.

The first thing to happen is that a person's heart stops beating. Lacking that power, their blood stops flowing around the body and their lungs stop drawing in breath. The exchange in their cells of oxygenated blood for deoxygenated blood, so vital for life, comes to a stop. Electrical energy in the brain ceases within about twenty seconds post-mortem, although it will take five minutes or so before the cells start to die.

The body then cools down until it reaches ambient temperature. This process is known as algor mortis. The blood stops moving around the body as livor mortis sets in. Thanks to gravity, blood pools nearest the ground, darkening the skin to a purplish-red colour. Rigor mortis follows, when the muscles start to stiffen as changes occur at a cellular level when the blood supply stops. The eyelids and the neck muscles are the first to be affected.

No longer held back by the body's natural defences, with the immune system not functioning, bacteria already in the body begin to take over. Bacterial action produces gases such as methane, hydrogen sulphide and ammonia, some of which travel through the arteries and veins that run throughout the body and create the effect known as marbling. The eyes bulge, and the tongue can swell and protrude from the mouth.

Other gases fill the body's cavities, creating the bloat stage as the body puffs up. The internal organs begin to decompose and the build-up of more gas starts to expel the liquid that results – a dark fluid will leak out of the body's orifices. Rich in nutrients, this liquid acts as a fertilizer – if the corpse is left uncovered in the open air, or buried in soil rather than in concrete, then healthy wild flowers and weeds will grow profusely around it.

Out in the open, flies will seek out the corpse and lay eggs in places such as the ears, nasal cavities and mouth. Maggots will hatch, depending on the species and conditions, and feed on the flesh of the body. Scavengers, drawn by the smell of decomposition, will come and gnaw at exposed parts of the corpse. This process can take anywhere from three to four days after death, to a few weeks, depending on the weather conditions and the environment the body has been placed in.

The final stages of decomposition involve the skin, loosened by the internal putrefaction, detaching from the muscles and skeleton. It too will be subject to scavenger attack and rot. If the temperature is a steady ten degrees Celsius, and the environment is relatively benign, then the whole process should take about twelve weeks or so, until just a skeleton remains.

How do we know all this? Because doctors and

scientists have, over the centuries, made it their business to understand the stages of death, to get a clear picture of what happens, as they also try to unravel what it is to be alive. Death is clearly a lot easier to figure out.

These days, specialist places exist which set out to aid our understanding of the processes of death. They're all in the US (although there is also one in Australia, but none in the UK) and have been given the not very cheery name of 'body farms'. Attached to universities, these body farms are facilities where scientists try to establish how bodies decompose in a wide variety of different circumstances. Their findings help provide accurate information to law enforcement officers around the globe towards understanding exactly how long a corpse might have been buried in a variety of different materials – mud or sand, for example.

Individuals who donate their bodies to these institutions can also specify (if they wish) exactly where and how they will be placed. Some bodies are simply left in cars; or in fridges; or outside, to see what effect the actions of scavengers have on being able to identify remains. As a result of the generosity of these people, so many professionals, whether in the police force, other agencies, or in my line of work, are learning all the time.

My knowledge of what can happen to a body postmortem deepened significantly when I presented a four-part special of *The Investigator*, which centred on the case of a missing woman, Carole Packman, who disappeared in 1985. Her husband, Russell, told their daughter she'd walked out on them. Russell had moved his new girlfriend, Patricia Causley, into the family home before Carole went missing and also took Patricia's surname as his own.

A decade later, Causley tried to fake his own death to claim the life insurance. He was convicted and sentenced to jail, then was also convicted of Carole's murder (although he still refuses to tell their daughter what happened). The police cannot explain what he did with her body, which has never been found. They told me and the team producing the TV programme that it's not possible to burn a body in the garden (which is what we believed he did) – you need a furnace, as that's the only way to get rid of teeth, joints, bones and so on.

However, I decided to try an experiment. Firstly, we spoke to an expert in the US, who burns bodies in all kinds of different scenarios. He told us that it *is* possible to burn a body in its entirety, until there's nothing left – just some brittle bones that can be broken up – on a domestic fire in the garden. You have to keep turning it over but it will all be gone in about six to seven hours.

To test what he was saying, we burned the corpse of a pig (in terms of density, pigs are similar to humans, we were told) on an open fire, which can reach temperatures close to 1,000 degrees Celsius. He was right – after a period of time, the body was all gone. Dorset Police were absolutely certain that the killer could not have burned Carole Packman's body in its entirety, but we showed that it was certainly possible.

Historically, the CPS has been reluctant to prosecute a murder without a body, but that has changed now. A notorious case in recent years was the murder of April Jones in October 2012. The five-year-old girl from Machynlleth, Wales, was killed by a neighbour who then burned her body in the open fire at his home. Police found bone fragments in the grate, and even though he'd tried to hide as much evidence as possible, it was the discovery of traces of her blood on the underside of the carpet in the living room that was the clincher in convicting him.

In some of the cases I've taken on, there is no DNA to examine, and we're left to use more traditional investigative methods, but there is a certainty about DNA evidence that pleases a jury and it's always good to have certainty as far as they're concerned.

In the Carole Packman case, a handwriting expert identified documents supposedly signed by Carole Packman as actually signed by Patricia Causley, but evidence such as this is never as convincing as that of DNA in the minds of a jury. They can see the numbers stack up: the certainties of a DNA match run into the millions, but handwriting? However, that extra, supportive evidence from a handwriting expert remains vital, because it tells more of the story. Fingerprint evidence is also a convincing item in terms of evidence; although it wasn't enough in the case of Andrew Kemp, believed to have killed a woman in Glasgow (see Chapter 10).

In some cases there is no DNA, no fingerprints – nothing forensic – for investigators to work from. There are always clear victims in these cases, but ones you never meet or talk to – they're children, being abused in photographs or in films. That offenders take these pictures always surprises me – who photographs themselves committing a crime? Who films themselves robbing a bank, or even murdering someone? No one. Rapists and, in particular, child abusers often film themselves carrying out the act, either to get pleasure from watching the footage at a later date or in order to distribute the film to other child abusers, occasionally for financial profit.

Some years ago, I went to a Crimes Against Children conference run by Interpol. Representatives from the Dutch police had brought with them a large database of images connected to offenders to show at the conference. Not of children being abused, but photographs taken at the same time and on the same reel of film or set of pictures. They wanted the attendees present, who had travelled from countries all over the world, to use these photographs to help identify offenders.

One featured an unusual lamp in the background; in another there was an umbrella in a beer garden. I suggested they put all these pictures into the public domain. When the police examine photographs for evidence, perhaps ten to twelve officers might review the images and what they can see in them. If they were to put those images into the public domain, at least 100,000 people might look at those details. Unfortunately, my suggestion wasn't followed up.

Interpol have started to post some pictures for the public to view, but in a limited way, and I think they need to go further. In the right circumstances, sharing evidence with the public has proven to be of assistance in the past: kidnapper and murderer Michael Sams was caught when the police released an audio tape of one of his telephone calls, and his ex-wife recognized his voice and informed the police. I always say the public are the eyes and ears of the police, and the best way of getting to the public is through the media – the media are the conduit for getting information out as widely as possible.

In my series *To Catch a Paedophile*, there was a case handled by the Metropolitan Police in 2004 where all that could be seen in an image, apart from a child being abused, was the back of a hand – nothing else that could identify the offender. However, even that is now something that science can use as an identifiable feature.

Dame Professor Sue Black at the University of Dundee was brought in for consultation. Her work is based upon the idea that the back – or 'dorsum' – of one hand is never identical to another. In much the same way as a fingerprint, there are enough individual indicators on a hand to mark it out as unique. Not even identical twins have identical dorsa. There are always features that are unique to each hand: freckles, vein patterns under the skin, scars, discolouration of the skin under the nail beds, creases around the knuckles and so on.

Fingerprints have helped solve crimes when the offender left no other evidence behind – or so they thought. Now, even if someone is forensically aware enough to avoid leaving evidence behind in the form of hair, DNA or fingerprints, if there are clear images of the backs of their hands in a photograph, this is a new forensic resource available to the police.

And so it proved with paedophile Dean Lewis Hardy, who was identified by the pattern of freckles on his hand. Once police had enough evidence to obtain a warrant, a search of his computer found the images matching those circulating on the internet. In 2009, after he had pleaded guilty, Hardy was sentenced to six years in jail. It was the first case to have used hand analysis in court to convict an offender.

Professor Black is building a database of photo-graphs of dorsa and hopes to be able to turn it into something searchable, as happened with fingerprints – and mugshots before that. She and her team work on thirty to fifty cases a year. Since she started this work in 2006, in all the cases that have come before the courts, once her analysis of the evidence has been shown to the offender, 82 per cent changed their plea to guilty.

This is only really possible thanks to meticulous and comprehensive analysis, and then employing detailed itemizing and filing systems. Ordering information is vital if you're going to identify offenders, but it relies on tremendously well maintained databases and these all have to be kept up to date, with new information entered at every stage of a major investigation. This relentless paperwork is one aspect of policing I am glad I no longer have to deal with. Not simply because it's paperwork, but because of what it represents – once something is in the system, there is an established list of ways to respond to it. Often, when an allegation is brought to the police, they will set out to investigate a crime, but I prefer to start off by finding out what the basis for the allegation is.

An allegation and a crime are two totally different things, and should be treated as such. However, the police tend to treat them as one and the same, as a statistic, and then they have a measurable unit to assess, quantify, investigate, discard or complete.

When somebody approaches me and asks me to investigate a case, one of the first things I do is investigate *them*. Who are they? What's their involvement? I'm clear with new clients about this. When they come to me, I tell them that I'll need to ask them some difficult questions, and one of those questions is about them being totally transparent. If they won't respond to that, then I explain that I can't help them.

Today, to give my mind time to absorb what I learn not just about the crime but also about the people involved, on all sides, I regularly step away from many of the investigations I'm working on. I'll only return to the files three weeks later to look again at the crime, having allowed things to sort themselves out in the recesses of my mind so that when I get back to the evidence I can see links and connections that I might have missed previously. I have information in my head I keep there – it might be there for ages, but I'll call it up and go, 'Yes, that bit fits there.' Of course, in the heat of a high-pressure investigation, an SIO can't do that.

This is where police reviews are particularly important. They are carried out now at specific stages of an investigation, each review an escalation from the previous one. The aim is sensible – to get a fresh pair of eyes looking at the evidence – but the success or failure of the process comes down to the quality of the review. What is the point of a review that just goes over what's been looked at and surmised before? The review of Jessie Earl's case (see Chapter 9) that identified the crime as a murder rather than a missing persons case is progress, but what happened in the previous reviews?

I'd like to see resources put into conducting more detailed and thorough reviews of all historic cases of missing people. How many of those 'missing' people from the seventies, eighties and nineties (I think these sorts of cases are handled differently – better – these days) are actually murder victims? Girls, pensioners, prostitutes – so many vulnerable women all disappeared and no one in authority seems to have minded? Take Pamela Exall, who disappeared off a beach in Norfolk in 1974. Was a serial killer like Peter Tobin responsible? There will always be people waiting for answers to questions such as this – families still wondering what happened to their child, their sibling. Knowing the predilections of some of the serial killers who *have* been arrested, it would be possible to narrow down the number of potential cases to review by grouping them into a relevant age bracket – say fourteen to thirty-five – and then investigate to see what, if anything, could be learned. Have these missing people been murdered?

The police handle crime scenes and carry out investigations in very different ways these days, but the criminals of today have also adapted their methods. This is what's known as 'the *CSI* effect', marking a change in crime scene awareness gleaned from the TV shows that spell out how the police carry out forensic work. It's led to ordinary criminals learning how to avoid being looked at, but funnily enough, it's those who prepare carefully to carry out a crime who are most at risk of being detected. The more planning they do, the greater the risk of them being caught. Opportunistic crimes, born out of spontaneity, can be the more successful ones as they are the hardest to solve.

Imagine you're planning to commit a crime. To carry out the research needed, you have to use the internet. Browsing on a computer at home, or even on a mobile phone, is too risky – both can easily be linked to you. Instead, you plan to use a public computer at a library or an internet café. If you intend to stay off the radar by looking things up in an internet café – half an hour away from your home, let's say – how will you get there? The card you pay with can be traced, and even if you pay in cash, your phone's SIM can give away your position.

If you travel by public transport, CCTV can be accessed at the stations you went through to verify your route. CCTV footage has improved so much over the years – ten to fifteen years ago the quality was poor and you'd probably be able to say that the figures in view were human but not much more. Now, however, everything is in HD. It would be difficult to avoid being identified anywhere where CCTV is in use, and in the UK there's a lot of it. Facial recognition software, though not yet widely used, is also particularly impressive.

If you decide to take to the road and travel somewhere to commit your crime, it's so much harder to operate in the way that serial killers of the past such as Peter Tobin or Angus Sinclair did. So many external factors have a bearing. As well as CCTV in train and bus stations, there's automatic number plate recognition (ANPR) software operating on many of the road networks, and mobile phone tracking can help to trace a suspect's movements – both in real time and from their data history.

When you become a suspect, the technology that collates information is so much better than it used to be, as a result of upgrades in HOLMES (Home Office Large Major Enquiry System; the database that links all the police forces' computer systems together so that they're all searchable from one point of entry). When the name of Peter Sutcliffe was logged on to the handwritten index cards that made up the databank of the Yorkshire Ripper inquiry team not once, but *nine* times, a number of murders might have been prevented if the police had been able to cross-reference those records properly. It wouldn't happen in this day and age because HOLMES is set up to cross-reference the names of witnesses, interviewees and suspects that come under the investigation team's gaze many times.

All these things add up, so using tradecraft helps you to see what should be avoided if you want to carry out a crime; just as it helps those who want to catch you.

Despite the *CSI* factor, technology continues to come to the aid of investigators. Almost everyone these days has some kind of online presence, some digital footprint that can be stored and studied. To assist me in the course of my investigations, I have access to a system called Tracesmart. It's a web-based programme that enables me to find individuals in the UK from single facts such as their date of birth, name, or the area in which they live.

Only certain people have access to Tracesmart, as it's open to abuse. Accordingly, I had to go through a strict vetting process. It collects information from the massive amounts of data people provide as they live their lives, from the electoral roll, online services such as utility companies, major shopping sites, film and TV streaming services – it's fairly comprehensive. Sometimes the information is out of date and you'll end up with a previous address, for example, but even that is a starting point. Searching is also harder when people have a common name, but it's still a pretty effective resource.

There are also websites where you can find out peoples' IP addresses, so while an email might appear anonymous to a casual user, knowing the IP address allows you to discover who hosted the site that sent it, and who owns it. Once you have that, you can usually obtain the location information pretty quickly.

Along with Tracesmart, open source search engines – ones open for you and me to use, such as Google – are also worth utilizing during the course of an investigation. You have to use as many of them as possible, and not rely on just one, because sites of information and search engines share information in myriad ways.

Social media – Facebook, Instagram, Twitter, Snapchat – all of these platforms are useful resources, and allow me to find out stuff about people either from their own pages or through their connections. People often post stuff without thinking about what it is they're writing or who's going to read it. Twitter in particular has helped me locate people, whether it be suspects, people of interest or witnesses, from their choice of language, references they make, the people they follow or areas they mention. They might even give something specific away in their biography, or they might post photographs that can be used to identify particular locations. They might even be foolish (or technologically naive) enough to leave GPS information in the metadata of photos they upload.

With all this technology to hand and with DNA profiling making it possible to match evidence from the crime scene to an offender, you'd have thought that the police would have no trouble identifying offenders and solving crimes. However, while technology is helpful, it also costs money. Conducting detailed examinations of phones or computers for sites visited, browser search terms, deleted or hidden images incurs a significant use of resources, meaning that lower priority crimes are ignored.

If I were to attend a crime scene as a police officer today, there might be, say, twenty cigarette butts left at the location – I would have to decide which one(s) to test. It wouldn't be possible to test them all. Even evidence that is seized after a search won't necessarily be sent for analysis. If, for example, ten hard drives are seized when a suspected paedophile's address is searched, the police will often have to decide which of them will merit full analysis. Policing is now no longer about collecting and analysing all potential evidence, it's about managing cost.

Along with financial shortages, I also feel the criminal justice system no longer threatens anyone enough not to carry out offences. If I commit a certain crime, what will happen if I'm caught? What are the chances of me getting caught in the first place? Who's going to catch me? Who is watching me? Will I lose my job? Will I go to jail? It's called cognitive distortion, the offender's justification for committing the crime. It's something we all do in our everyday lives, to some extent anyway. 'I was only doing 50 mph in a 40 mph zone, not 60';

'I only smoke five a day, not like my friend who smokes twenty.' The criminal version of this is, 'I was only looking at pictures of a twelve-year-old, she wasn't five'; 'I only touched her, it's not liked I raped her or anything.'

The sad fact is most criminals either are prepared to take those risks or aren't threatened by the consequences of being caught. Then there are the ones – fewer of them, thank goodness – who think they can get away with what they've done, because they feel they are above the law. That they're too rich, too successful, too famous to be considered an offender by the police. Which brings us to Jimmy Savile.

6

HIDING IN PLAIN SIGHT

JIMMY SAVILE DIED ON SATURDAY, 29 OCTOBER 2011.

Dame Esther Rantzen, the well-known broadcaster and founder of Childline, the counselling service for children, said he was 'knighted by the Queen, knighted by the Pope, fantastic charity fundraiser, which of course he was, he was all those things'.

'But,' she added, after the evidence shown in the TV programme I made about Savile was in the public domain, 'he was also a child abuser.'

Less than twelve months after Savile's death, Peter Watt, head of the NSPCC's helpline, described Savile as 'one [of] the most prolific sex offenders the NSPCC has ever come across'.

Following the broadcast of *Exposure: The Other Side of Jimmy Savile* in 2012, the Metropolitan Police launched an investigation into Savile's crimes. Ten weeks later, they announced that hundreds of people had been in contact. Dozens of crimes across seventeen police force areas were alleged to involve Savile as a suspect, while 80 per cent of those who came forward to report abuse were children or young people at the time of the incidents.

By March 2013, 214 complaints had been made against Savile after his death, which, had they been reported to the police at the time, would have been criminal offences. Four victims reported being raped by Savile when they were under the age of ten. Others reported serious sexual assaults by him, including another four who were also under ten years old. Savile had targeted boys as well as girls. It's not certain, but it's possible – from what it's been claimed he said, as well as evidence about his movements – that he even sexually abused corpses in a mortuary.

On 26 June 2014, UK Secretary of State for Health Jeremy Hunt delivered a public apology in the House of Commons to patients of the National Health Service who were abused by Savile.

'Savile was a callous, opportunistic, wicked predator who abused and raped individuals, many of them patients and young people, who expected and had a right to expect to be safe. His actions span five decades – from the 1960s to 2010. As a nation at that time we held Savile in our affection as a somewhat eccentric national treasure with a strong commitment to charitable causes. Today's reports show that in reality he was a sickening and prolific sexual abuser who repeatedly exploited the trust of a nation for his own vile purposes.'

I'm glad that Jimmy Savile's name will be recorded in the history books as that of a serial paedophile, a predatory abuser of children, and not that of an entertainer and DJ. I'm proud of the part I had to play in making that so. I make no bones about this. Whatever else Jimmy Savile did in his life, whatever he achieved for himself or for others, he's not worth remembering as anything other than what he was: a sex offender.

What should really be remembered, what should stand to represent what he was, are the stories of his victims, and the lives they had to piece together in the wake of his horrific abuse. That they have survived while everything about him has not – even the headstone on his grave (it was removed and destroyed after it had stood for only nineteen days) – is about as good as it gets, if you ask me. There's only one, small sour note for me. While it's good that Savile's victims have had the opportunity to speak out about what he did to them, and be believed, it's disappointing in this respect: ultimately, he got away with it. I'd love to have seen Savile at the Old Bailey, facing his demons, heading to jail.

The Savile programme started for me in an unusual way, because it involved two broadcasters. I was travelling back from visiting Interpol in Lyon, France, in

July 2011, with *Newsnight* (at that time, I did quite a lot of *Newsnight* reports) and Meirion Jones, an incredibly talented producer and journalist, for whom I have huge respect. On the way home, he said to me, out of the blue, 'Have you ever heard of Jimmy Savile being a weird bloke, being involved in child abuse?'

I thought for a moment, and said, 'No. I mean, he's weird, but I've never heard anything like that about him.'

'Apparently, he was arrested by the police,' Meirion said. 'I don't know whether it was your force or another force.'

'Well, I've never heard of it, but I'll see what I can find out,' I told him.

Rumours had buzzed around Savile for years, and he had always swatted them away. In 2000, when interviewed by Louis Theroux for his documentary strand *When Louis Met . . .* , Savile spoke about the 'salacious tabloid people' who had raised rumours about whether he was a paedophile, and he stated plainly, 'I know I'm not.'

Back home I made some enquiries and established that yes, Savile had been contacted by the police, and it *had* been my old force, Surrey Police, who interviewed him. My contact there, a former senior officer, told me that Savile had been formally questioned as part of a police investigation, so I reported back to Meirion.

'We're going to do something on it, as far as an investigation goes,' Meirion told me. 'We've got someone who's not a victim, but telling us about Savile's offending . . .'

At that point he went on to reveal what he'd been told about Savile. However, almost overnight, he called me back and said, 'They're not doing it. *Newsnight* are not doing it.'

I was incredibly surprised. Apparently, the story they wanted to run wasn't about whether or not Savile was a sex offender, but about the police's shortcomings: had they failed in their job in some way? Had they had their chance to investigate him properly and mucked it up? Had they been overawed by Savile's celebrity status?

I was baffled. Everybody – for other producers and lawyers made the same comment – was missing sight of the fact that it wasn't about police failures, it was about him being a paedophile. Jimmy Savile – friend of Prime Minister Thatcher, charity fundraiser, and all the other things he was known for – was a paedophile. That's the point of all of this.

I spoke to Meirion Jones again. 'Let me take this away and see what I can do.'

With his blessing, I took the idea to ITV and said to the team I met there, 'There's a really interesting story here, but we'd have to handle it incredibly carefully. It will take time and we'd have to be very secretive.'

Naturally, the bigwigs at ITV were concerned and we had numerous meetings with lawyers. We sat in the main boardroom for hours, talking it through, but eventually Alex Gardiner, a friend and executive producer, said, 'Look, Mark, I think you're right. I think there's something here. Let's run with it.'

You have to remember, Savile had only just died – in the public's mind, he was still a hero.

So it was a brave decision to make, given none of us at the time – least of all myself – knew how things were going to turn out. We started working on the idea and at first it was just the two of us – my producer Lesley Gardiner (without whom the programme would never have been made – and no relation to Alex) and I. We started to dig away, keeping everything firmly under wraps.

We advised the board at ITV that we weren't going to give them regular updates, and that all feedback would be limited. We didn't tell anyone about what we were uncovering, who we were speaking to, and nothing went on the ITV intranet. I made some suggestions as to how we could limit circulation of our papers, because as each day passed and we learned a little bit more, I started to get a sense of how big this was going to be – to some degree. I could never have anticipated quite how big, but I knew it was going to be a major story.

I was certain that there was something buried in

Savile's past, waiting to be uncovered. My instinct turned out to be right: in fact, our programme totally inverted the public's perception of him. Overnight, in people's minds he went from being the *Jim'll Fix It* guy to a predator stalking victims in hospitals and television studios up and down the land.

It wasn't easy at the outset. While there were many who felt we should investigate wherever the evidence took us, a lot of other people at ITV were more wary. I told Lesley that we weren't going to fail, and whatever had to happen to get the broadcast made, we would get it done.

Early on in our investigation, Lesley came into the office and said, 'Watch this.'

She turned the TV to a news report about an auction of Savile's personal items. Some of his things were selling for hundreds of thousands of pounds – his car, a Rolls-Royce, was a star item in the sale.

As we watched the auction unfold, I remember saying to her, 'Do you know what? In a year's time, those things are going to be of absolutely no value at all.'

That was the moment when I felt that there was a really important programme to be made, not because we would be accusing a dead man of having carried out serious sexual abuse, but because what we were setting out to prove would change a culture. No longer would people be able to turn a blind eye to and pretend they hadn't seen what they'd just witnessed; now, victims would be believed. I'd never been in a position where the stakes were so high, and I knew how important it was to get the story out there.

The first issue we had to address was that of credibility, and it meant we had to carry out some serious due diligence. I told one of the newspapers that interviewed me later, long after the programme had been broadcast, that I ran the story as if I was running a criminal investigation. The same tests had to be applied. Can we obtain good evidence? Can we corroborate that evidence? Does each piece of evidence back up the others, or does one contradict the others? The same level of security required around a criminal investigation was also essential; Lesley and I kept a lot of the evidence I gathered on paper only, not on computers, so that the identities of the people we spoke to could be kept a close secret.

We already knew that Savile had been spoken to by Surrey Police some years earlier. In 2007, he had been interviewed under caution by officers investigating an allegation of indecent assault in the 1970s at the now-closed Duncroft Approved School for Girls near Staines, Surrey, where he was a regular visitor. The CPS advised there was insufficient evidence to take any further action and no charges were brought.

The following year, the *Sun* linked Savile to child abuse at the Jersey children's home Haut de la Garenne. Initially, he denied visiting the home, but then had to back down and admit he had done so when the paper published a photograph showing him there, surrounded by children. The States of Jersey Police issued a statement, saying that an allegation of an indecent assault by Savile at the home in the 1970s had been investigated, but there had been insufficient evidence to proceed.

As we continued in our research, Lesley and I held a few meetings with people about the progress of our work. I couldn't get my head round the fact that it seemed only Alex, Lesley and I thought the big story was that Savile was a paedophile, not that the police had failed to investigate him properly. So many still believed that, instead of identifying him for what he was, the story was that the authorities had messed it up. Why can't people see that, I kept asking Lesley? They were looking for failure from the institutions, rather than the abuse carried out by someone cleverly hiding it from those very institutions.

Maybe it was because people still wanted to see Savile as the flamboyant entertainer, the how's-about-that-then man, and couldn't yet believe all the things we were starting to prove against him. Or maybe it was the fear of what might come as a result of exposing such a famous individual.

The first person I managed to speak to regarding Savile's abuse had been in touch with Meirion while Savile was alive, but she was still frightened to talk about him now that he was dead. It was clear that what this person was saying about being abused by Savile was credible, but at that time hers was a lone voice – I would need others to speak up if I was going to get any kind of inquiry off the ground. Although this person was instrumental in kick-starting my investigation, it became clear that this was going to be a difficult one. There was so much fear in talking about Savile, still.

At first I found this mystifying. However, as time went on I was able to understand it more. The people who were still scared when he was dead, how could they possibly have coped when he was alive? Savile was a nasty piece of work when he wanted to be – he had a past to which he'd often allude, referring to his mates who were handy with guns. He was also incredibly litigious, and if he'd still been alive and heard even the faintest noise about an investigation into his private life, we'd have never got it broadcast. He'd have sued everybody from the boardroom to the doorman, and his victims wouldn't have dared to come forward and be named – they'd have been too frightened of dealing with the repercussions of his anger.

Lesley and I had already agreed how we would keep the information, the testimonies we were obtaining, confidential. I think it's because we were able to demonstrate our processes to that first person I spoke to that I was able to find another person willing to talk to me about what had happened to her. The answers to my questions made it clear to me that what they both separately recalled had in fact happened. And the link between the two women was the residential school they'd both attended: Duncroft.

Duncroft was a school for girls who had failed in mainstream education and were considered to be emotionally disturbed in some way. If you google the name of the school, the first page of search results is a clear indication of what we found – you don't need to go any further. 'A paedophile sweetshop', 'Savile abused 23', 'Savile carried out 46 assaults'. Staff who worked at the school, or with Savile in his offices, had a similar story to tell about why they felt he had an untouchable aura about him: his charitable work for the hospitals he supported, his association with Margaret Thatcher and his links to the Royal Family. It all made it impossible for those people to face up to the fact that something was very wrong, even though he was carrying out his attacks right under their noses.

And this is exactly what he was doing. He'd come to the school, take girls out in his car and force himself on them. Or he'd do what he wanted in the privacy of the room he was given use of in the school. One of the women I spoke to told me, 'He had an alcove in his dressing room that had a curtain over it and he would take you behind the curtain. There were no staff around in the room, just the girls in there and one or two other people.'

If the girls tried to tell anyone what he'd done, they were never believed. Another woman I spoke to said that she'd tried to tell members of staff what had happened to her but they punished her for speaking out.

'I was taken upstairs to the isolation unit, left there for two or three days and told that I could come back into the building when I refrained from saying such filthy things and retract the accusations and, you know, that was it. When I came out I just didn't say anything more because I hated it in the isolation unit, it was a padded cell.'

This was Savile's thing: to focus on children society had pushed to the margins, and to do so in places where he could get away with what he wanted without the glare of publicity. Whether it was disabled children, patients in secure hospitals, or pupils in schools for children considered in some way unfit for the mainstream, these individuals were available to him for exploitation without his having to justify his presence to any authority.

It's all so obvious to us now, but it wasn't then. At that time, Jimmy Savile was the man who apparently cared about the well-being of children others didn't pay much attention to, or even want to think about.

I found a third woman who, like the others, had suffered at the hands of Savile at Duncroft. The interviews I carried out with all three victims were shocking to me then. It was clear their experiences with Savile had had a huge impact on their lives. Two of them agreed not only to go on camera but also to waive their anonymity and speak out for the first time. Given the details they were prepared to reveal, and how frightened they were, it was an incredibly brave decision.

I was then told about a possible witness to an assault by Savile in Leeds which, if true, would be vital to the investigation, because it expanded not only our view of where Savile offended, but also the nature of his offending. It took the focus away from Duncroft, and the witness claimed they actually saw Savile carrying out an indecent assault on a fourteen-year-old girl. I spoke to as many people as I could track down who might help me confirm this account and perhaps provide more information about other possible assaults by Savile. Each time, I would ask my questions, designed to encourage them to trust me, to know that they could talk to me in confidence, and I'd make sure they knew that if they were aware of anyone else I could contact, they should tell me.

I spent days, weeks, even months communicating with a number of women. Sometimes I would talk to them for a long time before it became clear that no offence had actually taken place. Tracking some of them down was a challenge, as many had married and changed their names, often moving away from the area in which they grew up – especially those who had been in care. So many were so reluctant to talk at first. The change in the environment for victims of abuse to speak out, from then to now, is astonishing.

After I'd been working on the investigation for some weeks, it became clear that a number of people had harboured suspicions about Savile during his life-time and either were not believed or were unable to provide credible evidence. Rumours circulated; and while there were some individuals who acted on those rumours, others were unable to succeed in getting any kind of authority to take them seriously.

One who could, and did, was the former chairman of BBC Children in Need. Sir Roger Jones said he had heard things that led him to believe Savile was 'a pretty creepy kind of character' and so decided that he didn't want Savile involved with the charity. He went so far as to ban Savile from taking part in any-thing to do with the appeals run by Children in Need.

Rumour was all he needed to do this: 'If you're going to go on the attack and make claims against [Savile] then you'd need evidence – hard evidence that simply wasn't there. But if you're protecting yourself you can do that without evidence.' Yet no one else at the BBC thought to listen to these rumours, or to take action against Savile appearing with children on *Jim'll Fix It* – or for him to stop appearing on BBC's *Top of the Pops*.

In today's world, where there are multiple plat-forms for listening to music and watching bands perform, it's hard to explain how important *Top of the Pops* was as a programme in its heyday. Fifteen million people watched every week. If you were a teenager in the 1970s, it was the only chance you had to watch the acts behind the music you liked. And, unlike other shows where the bands performed just for the cameras, on *Top of the Pops* there was a live studio audience mingling with the artists, dancing around the stage at the feet of the performers.

Securing a place in the TV studio audience was a glamorous aspiration for thousands of teenagers across the country. The reality – being shunted around a cavernous studio to stand in front of a stage where a band would mime their way through their hit record – was almost certainly anything but. Perhaps the only time to feel excited was if the camera picked you out among the dancers, so you could wave to your family and friends watching at home, or if the DJ presenting the programme decided to stand next to you, his arm slung over your shoulder as he (and in the 1970s it was almost always a he) introduced the next act. Unless, of course, you were unlucky enough to be on the show the week it was presented by Jimmy Savile.

I identified a separate group of women who came to know Savile as a result of being in the audience on *Top of the Pops*. This was significant, because of their ages; although you were meant to be fifteen years old to attend, many audience members were only there

because they could pass for that age. One BBC producer I spoke to told me that he once met Savile with a
girl the producer believed could only be about twelve
years old. Savile told the producer he'd met her while
presenting *Top of the Pops*; and that he then spent the
night with her.

Two of the women who'd been in the *Top of the Pops*
audience at that time both agreed to be interviewed
on camera. They were still both incredibly scared to
speak out, even after all these years. Combined with
their current circumstances, this meant we needed to
carefully conceal their identities during filming. I won't
give away exactly how I came to find them because
doing so would expose the very people I said I would
protect.

Both women talked about meeting Savile when
they were fifteen years old. One described how he had
full sexual intercourse with her at that age, and the
other said he had sex with her when she was sixteen
years old. She never consented to this and she now
considers it rape. They went on to give accounts of
multiple sexual assaults perpetrated by Savile and
told me they both contracted a sexually transmitted
disease from him.

The production team and I were careful not to
speak in detail about their accounts of abuse before we
interviewed these women. It was important that they
told us their experiences as they recalled them, so that

if there was overlap in their accounts, or other points of similarity, that was because it came from Savile and his behaviour – and not from us. I had no idea the two women who made allegations of rape were going to disclose accounts of such serious assaults. Although I've heard many accounts of child sexual abuse during my career as an investigator, the production team and I all found these accounts particularly upsetting. So much so that Lesley and I spoke a lot over the days following the interviews about how emotional we had found them, and how we would look to support everyone involved – crew as well as witnesses.

Using all the techniques and skills I've developed over my many years as a detective and now as an investigative reporter, I carried on searching for people who might offer further avenues of research for our programme, and gathered testimony from people who could have information about Savile's activities in the past. This resulted in me speaking to celebrities who had worked with him, people in the media who had interviewed him, as well as individuals who were now adults but who had met him as children.

Among those I spoke with, there were others who alleged abuse, and by the end of our investigation five people agreed to go on camera and tell their stories. I don't believe I did anything special to persuade them to talk to us; we offered them the opportunity to share what they had kept to themselves for years, tested what we could of their accounts, and kept accumulating material for our programme.

I continued to discuss with Lesley the security of our research. I didn't want the fact that I was undertaking an investigation into Jimmy Savile to get out to the media. Even though it might have been advantageous to us to have other people made aware they could come forward to speak to me about their experiences with him, we didn't need the extra difficulties we would face if word got out to Savile's supporters that we were looking into his past in this fashion. That would only scare off potential new interviewees and it might also force those to whom we'd already spoken to retract their statements.

It's incredible to look back at the need for such hush-hush now – Savile's name is, as I said before, forgotten in every respect other than as a notorious paedophile – but in the months following his death he was still regarded as a national treasure. The usual difficulties of investigating an historical crime – the lack of corroborating evidence, the reliability of witnesses' memories – were compounded by the fact we were dealing with someone whose reputation was seemingly so untouchable that I was still unsure, even the weekend before the programme was due to air, whether or not it would be broadcast.

The material we'd gathered was shown to a leading barrister, Ian Glen, QC (who has sadly passed away), to see if it would pass the evidentiary threshold. Ian's verdict was that what the complainants were speaking about amounted to a pattern of offending. There was independence between two or three groups of complainants and the detail of their accounts was backed up to some extent by independent witnesses who observed relevant occasions of misconduct. It was his opinion that the evidence he had seen would amount to reasonable grounds for Savile's arrest had he still been alive.

This is what we needed to hear. We'd gone beyond whispered rumours to something more substantial. If Savile had been alive it would have amounted to a court case. Of course, nothing had ever gone to court when he was alive; the investigation in 2007 by Surrey Police had never resulted in anything, least of all a prosecution. Although Surrey Police stated it was based on a single complaint relating to Duncroft, we know that at least two women were subsequently interviewed, and statements were taken by the police, as part of this inquiry.

The run-up to the broadcast of our programme was quite the whirlwind. We'd kept our cards close to our chest – up to this point we had shared very little information beyond our small production team and few people outside this little circle were fully aware of what was about to air. When it was time for ITV's lawyers and those at the top of the hierarchy to see the film, we started to get an inkling of how big it was going to be.

Out of earshot of the rest of the team, Lesley and I had a brief conversation. We didn't want to alarm anyone with our thoughts at this late stage, but she said, 'You know, we'll either work in television for a long time, or we'll never work again.'

We were on a precipice. Everything could come crashing down around our ears and we really felt that. The stakes were so high.

As we entered the final stages of post-production, a story broke in the press that ITV were looking at screening a programme in relation to Jimmy Savile's private behaviour. BBC Radio Leeds were very supportive of Savile – he was a Leeds man. The radio station ran a phone-in, which I listened to because I thought someone might phone up with a crucial piece of information. Actually, all they did was criticize me. It wasn't the first time I'd received public criticism, but it was particularly emotive, and the virulence of some people's feelings was shocking.

I was still working from the mindset of a former policeman and investigative journalist; I saw things in detail, so my point of view was quite focused. Suddenly, we were being asked to consider the big picture and how our film would play out at a national level.

The weekend before the programme went out, I was worried. I was seriously concerned about how it was going to be received. I thought, 'You know what? If the public don't go with this, if the media don't go with this, I'll be hung out to dry.' The pressure on the team that final weekend was intense and I can't pretend that I didn't find it stressful. At that point, I replied to questions from the newspapers wanting some sort of insight into the programme before it was shown, by saying, 'I know some people will have fixed views and they won't be changed – but all I would ask is that you watch the programme before you make your mind up.'

The documentary that was eventually broadcast on 3 October 2012 was the culmination of almost a year's work, which had taken Lesley, our production team and me up and down the country and on a rollercoaster of emotions. Hearing intensely shocking accounts of child sexual abuse which had clearly had a huge impact on people's lives was one thing; it was another to be toppling the memory of a person such as Savile at the same time.

The reaction to the broadcast of our programme was extraordinary. As the story started to evolve over the subsequent days, the articles in the national press (broadsheets as well as tabloids) and conversations on television and radio shows brought home how much of an impact the programme had, not just on the victims (and many other people who came forward as a result of the broadcast) but on the public generally.

The BBC were criticized in a number of places for having continued to employ Savile and for going ahead with tribute programmes while there were question marks over his conduct. They mishandled their treatment of the row over axing the story from *Newsnight* badly, and heads rolled at various levels – including the Director-General – as an extensive and incredibly expensive inquiry established the flawed decision-making process within the BBC.

My mum rang me, concerned about the danger I might be in as the sparks flew in the days immediately after the broadcast. I reassured her that I'd be fine. I neglected to add that the anger we'd provoked from some corners – for exposing a criminal paedophile – made me want to do my job even more.

The great shame is that Savile was not around to face the allegations. In some ways I understand why he had managed to avoid being held to account while he was alive – though I think some divisions of the press who were powerful and financially robust enough could have taken him on. In my eyes, the police were at fault when they had him under investigation in 2007 but failed to follow through with it properly. It would have been gratifying to see him face justice. It's a consolation to believe that we were right to have tackled such a highly sensitive subject, and to have given to the women he abused a voice that so many of them had been denied as children.

As a result of our investigation into Savile, some power has been given back to victims. Not just his victims, but other victims of historic sexual abuse. We've changed public attitudes. I don't think there's been a programme in the last ten – maybe even twenty – years that has had such an impact. For forty-one days, news about Savile, sparked by the programme, sat on the front pages of newspapers.

Not only has it changed attitudes, it's changed legislation.

It's given a voice to people out there who never felt confident enough to speak up, and it's put away some particularly dangerous offenders. Not just the ones we know about from the papers – that is, the high-profile ones – but others up and down the country.

There are offenders out there guilty of historic child sex offences and those individuals know exactly what they've done. What I'd say to them, and I've said it many times, is that I hope you sleep very, very lightly at night, fearful that the next bang on the door is going to be the police. I hope that the law one day catches up with all of them. Sadly, I don't think it will, but we can at least chip away.

Being a victim of any crime is horrific. Being a victim of a personal crime such as a sexual offence – particularly if you have your innocence taken away from you as a child – changes your life. The biggest travesty for me was that so many people who had concerns about his behaviour and proclivities, people who had the ability to stop him from having access to children, didn't do anything.

Why did one arm of the BBC, Children in Need, stop him, but not another? If he's not safe on your programmes, he's not safe on anyone else's, surely? And how was it possible for Savile to be given the freedom to roam hospitals such as Stoke Mandeville and Broadmoor, to have his own rooms, his own set of keys? What the hell was going on? Why were senior managers allowing a bloke like this to walk around with female prisoners? I hope we gave those people restless nights after our broadcast.

Following the furore around Savile, the police opened an investigation into historical child abuse crimes, Operation Yewtree. People who thought the offences they had committed in the sixties and seventies were forgotten about were made to think again as celebrity after celebrity was interviewed and – with the proper proof, presented and tested in court – brought to justice. Stuart Hall, Rolf Harris and Max Clifford were among them.

Victims who had long given up hope of ever being believed about what had been done to them when they were children suddenly found that not only were there people prepared to listen to them, but there was also a willing interest from the authorities to take those allegations seriously and investigate them. It's hard to overestimate how extraordinary a feeling that must be – to have had no one care for decades about what you said had happened, only to have someone finally listen, pay attention and do something about it.

Society has a big role to play, because we created these monsters. We created opportunities for them. After all, offending is all about access and opportunity. A paedophile has to have access to a child, and an opportunity to offend and get away with it. In the case of Rolf Harris, Max Clifford and Jimmy Savile, these things were handed to them on a plate.

Once you start looking at the issue this way, it changes almost everything you think about the way an offender has been perceived in the past. For instance, we'll never know whether *Jim'll Fix It* was a vehicle Savile created for his offending, or whether it was just luck as far as he was concerned. Once you start to think like an offender, it's hard not to believe the worst of everything they've said or done.

Despite the pride I felt at what the programme achieved, numerous people had a go at me personally about it, and the effect it had on Savile's 'legacy'. Some particularly horrible comments were made about me on social media. The increase in that sort of abuse, I think, has come about because users can be anonymous. It's incredible what some people will say: this man should be killed, this man should be hanged. I was sent photoshopped images of me being hanged, I was sent child abuse material, I was even sent a petrol bomb. I received death threats.

It's really quite hard to deal with, but it's the reality of the world I inhabit, and not just as a result of the Savile investigation. During and after *On the Run*, the programme in which I caught wanted criminals, who were then put away for a long time – those people, their friends and relatives all made various threats towards me.

Those who know me – colleagues in both the police and journalism – understand that I have always been dedicated to exposing wrongdoing, and through the work I've done around child protection I tackled issues so many turned a blind eye to. The critics say the past is the past, and that the memory of Savile should be left alone. Should it? Does that mean whatever has happened in the past – if it relates to someone who is dead – should be ignored and never questioned? Try telling that to an historian. Try telling that to a victim of historic sexual abuse.

It's not only in the field of historic crimes that we have seen a seismic shift in attitudes surrounding child sexual abuse. In the aftermath of the Savile documentary, while many hundreds – if not thousands – of victims across the UK gained the confidence to come forward and report the abuse they had suffered many years previously as children, countless others were also able to talk about more recent offences. The CPS has adopted a much more determined approach to charging offenders with crimes that, years ago, they might not have considered prosecuting. Since the Savile exposé, the actions of the Metropolitan Police show how determined officers are to follow up every lead and to catch offenders – no matter how powerful they are.

However, the impact of unmasking Savile took a dangerous turn, I felt. In the course of my investigation of him, I carefully collected victims' accounts to build up a catalogue of compelling testimonies. All the time I was aware that my evidence needed to be tested at the level I would expect to see before taking it to court, because Savile was dead and unable to defend himself.

Investigations into other individuals stopped seeming like the sorts of investigations I knew, and became instead some sort of free-for-all trawl through the nation's past. In the summer of 2015, former Prime Minister Sir Edward Heath was dragged into the controversy when his name was released in bizarre circumstances as being linked to child sexual abuse offences.

On 3 August, the Independent Police Complaints Commission (IPCC) announced that Wiltshire Police had had an allegation referred to them by a former senior police officer. In late 2014, the officer had told Wiltshire Police that he believed a trial in the 1990s had been halted because information came to light that Heath was involved in the abuse of children. Wiltshire Police said that they made the referral to the IPCC in March, 'having worked tirelessly to establish the facts of the allegation'. Apparently, the IPCC sat on this information for five months before making the public announcement.

On the same day that the IPCC made the referral public, a Wiltshire Police superintendent stood outside Heath's former home and made a statement to the press: 'This is an appeal for victims: in particular, if you have been the victim of any crime from Sir Ted Heath or any historical sexual offences, or you are a witness or you have any information about this, then please come forward.'

It is normally only after the courts have determined the guilt of a living suspect that the police appeal for victims to come forward, or (when the alleged offender is deceased), the CPS has considered all the evidence and has decided that the person would have been charged had they been alive. By directly appealing for victims, the police were sending a clear message that they had already decided the former prime minister was guilty of sex crimes.

This obviously raises the question of what enquiries Wiltshire Police and the IPCC had made in the many months each had to establish the truth, because within forty-eight hours of the press statement, the media had figured out who the prosecutor and the defendant were in the trial in the 1990s that had been halted. Both the prosecutor's account and that of the defendant confirmed that the case had been dropped – but not because of a cover-up or political inference, or indeed any kind of conspiracy, but because some of the prosecution witnesses had refused to attend court.

So why did the IPCC and Wiltshire Police make public this clearly unsubstantiated and incorrect complaint? When Wiltshire Police made their press statement, there was no direct allegation that was substantiated by evidence, or supported by a witness or another victim. Overwhelmingly, the allegations they had were third-party reports.

Later, it emerged that earlier that year, in April, the Metropolitan Police had received an allegation of rape against Heath, but decided there were 'no lines of enquiry that could proportionately be pursued'.

Naming individuals as potential offenders before they've been charged is a thorny issue. Obviously, Sir Edward Heath was dead, so that was never going to apply in his case, but in the wake of the Savile investigation, I believe there were occasions when it was right to name a suspect when preliminary investigations had taken place, and where there was plenty of substantial supporting evidence. Such an approach was crucial in helping to convict Max Clifford, Rolf Harris and Stuart Hall, for example, and the release of their names was done after the police had a number of victims making allegations. Where no such supporting evidence exists, however, where there is a paucity of credible witnesses, it seems inflammatory to me to name someone as guilty of an offence so reviled as paedophilia.

In that summer of 2015, it became apparent that a small number of journalists and well-placed individuals, including a few politicians, were determined to be at the forefront of attempts to establish that a significant number of well-organized paedophile rings existed, involving politicians both former and current. Sadly, the work of these individuals was not evidence-focused. Instead, they preferred to pass off rumour as fact and, incredibly worryingly in a few cases, put pressure on victims of child abuse, which led those victims to name high-profile people as offenders. And yet, even after public appeals for victims of organized political paedophile rings to come forward, many such victims remain sole complainants. This has made it easy for them to be described as fantasists; but while they may have made up or misremembered some aspects of what occurred in their childhood, I think their evidence should be tested before being discounted – or acted upon.

A contact of mine told me about one such complainant. That complainant is now under investigation himself but even though he previously put forward many lurid and fantastical suggestions of abuse at the hands of famous people during the 1970s, I think it was likely this man was abused when he was younger – just probably not by the men he named. Unfortunately, the police decided to declare his allegations 'credible and true', which I regard as a serious mistake. Credibility and truth are matters the courts are best placed to pass judgement on; it's not for the police to say whether the accusations are 'true'. Their job is to investigate the claims, gather evidence, present them to the CPS (or whoever is in charge at that time), and then leave it in the hands of the court to determine guilt.

This particular witness initially talked to the police and the media about being abused by Savile, but the way he described Savile approaching him, and then abusing him, felt off to me. I'd spoken to many of Savile's victims by that point and I knew how he operated, how brazenly he acted with them. What this witness described – how he'd been picked up and what had taken place – didn't seem to me to have happened.

Once this man started talking about group activities, and how he had been drawn into this select circle of abusers as one of their victims, I felt even less convinced.

Rarely acknowledged is how child sex offenders operate. Remember, the more people who know about an individual's offending, the far greater the risk of that person being exposed and caught, especially if they're well known or wealthy. Now think of the particularly strong position an offender would be in if they were to have information on a political or high-profile co-offender.

I've worked in the field of child sex offenders for nearly all my professional career. I can tell you that while there are always exceptions to the rule, abusers overwhelmingly offend in isolation and target victims known to them. For example, Savile operated with a handful of co-offenders (fewer than four), but he was very select, and on those occasions they were never with groups of other perpetrators. However, nearly all the allegations being made against political figures, past and present, from all the sources who have made them, are alleged to have occurred in group situations.

I was often asked by the press to comment on the allegations made by the complainant mentioned above, but I never did. I always felt that what he was telling everyone was going to backfire on him at some point. Sadly, when people come forward with false allegations, it can have the unfortunate effect of discrediting the evidence of actual victims.

I met regularly with Yewtree officers over the years and we shared information. I'd also frequently get calls from ITV executives who wanted to use a particular presenter on a programme and needed to check with me whether they were safe to do so. If I'd not heard anything about that person yet, I'd tell them to go ahead.

Although one time I was appearing on *Good*

Morning Britain and Max Clifford was brought on air shortly after me. The day after the Savile programme was broadcast, I'd had a message from someone Clifford had abused, so I knew even then that things were going to unravel for him. I remember thinking to myself, 'You're going to get nicked soon.'

As to the suggestion of high-profile figures forming paedophile rings, I have no doubt that over the years politicians have abused children, but I find it difficult to believe that they were able to operate in groups with impunity and without any knowledge of their actions ever being made public. Remember how many people were aware of rumours about one man – Savile? Imagine applying that to a disparate, even large group – how could so many individuals have kept those sort of rumours suppressed?

Unfortunately, just like murderers, paedophiles are at large in our society. Sometimes they seek out employment that will give them access to children, sometimes they will find other ways to approach their victims. I don't believe that any one occupation is more prone to being open to child abusers than any other. Huge strides in making it possible for victims to come forward – mostly the feeling that their testimony will be listened to, properly – have been made since the Savile story broke, but it's important that this progress isn't derailed by messy, unprovable hearsay and gossip. Evidence – and facts – is the way ahead.

Abusers like Savile make themselves everyone's friend, or at least try to. Parents, children, charity organizers and TV companies were all fooled by him. Some abusers don't bother with all that, and simply aim to persuade one important group that they are their friends, that they alone can be trusted. That group is, of course, their target: children.

7

THE CHURCHYARD

USUALLY WHEN I TAKE ON A CASE, I HAVE TO PIECE together a picture of the person I'm investigating – from families, police files and sometimes from autopsies. When the victim is a young person – a child or a teenager – it's never a vivid portrait, only a snapshot of who they were in the moments before they met their violent end. I deal with words on a page, moments glimpsed in family photographs, grim crime scene images, post-mortem reports, heart-rending memories written down as bald statements of fact. It always provokes a sadness in me, not knowing how someone looked when they were alive and well, out with their friends; laughing, smiling at their mum or dad over their breakfast before they left the house for school; all the things that made them who they were.

Sometimes, it's hard to remember that the people whose cases I investigate were living their lives fully on the day they died, thinking of their day ahead. If they hadn't met some sad end, there's every chance they would have gone on to lead full and long lives, doing the things we all do year after year until we grow old. Instead, they become fixed in time at the age they died and, for the parents of a child, that's how they will remain. Sometimes parents are unable to move on from the death of a child, and the child's room is preserved, never changing. That year's posters are never taken down to be replaced by something more grown up, new clothes are never hung in the wardrobe, new friends never sit on the bed to chat.

That's how it was in the case of Lee Boxell – until recently. Fifteen for ever, his posters of Sutton United football team still hang on his bedroom walls, but there are now toys belonging to his younger sister's children amongst the teenager's belongings. Lee left his home in Cheam on the morning of Saturday, 10 September 1988; his mum and dad, Christine and Peter, knew he was going off to watch the football. Sutton were playing away that afternoon so Lee had decided to go to see two other south London teams, Millwall and Charlton, play at Crystal Palace's ground, Selhurst Park. Lee met up with a friend that Saturday morning and, after spending a couple of hours together, they went off in different directions. Lee, so he told his friend, was heading to the football.

Another friend saw him, still in Sutton town centre, at the north end of the High Street, at about 2.20 p.m.

Kick-off was at 3 p.m. and it's a twenty-minute train journey from Sutton to the station nearest Selhurst Park, a stadium he'd never been to, which would have left him almost no time to make it there. Something must have made him change his mind about going to the match, but what that was, no one ever found out, because Lee was never seen again.

In an era before mobile phones, Lee was conscientious about contacting his parents when he was out, calling home from a pay phone when he thought he might be late back. That day, Christine and Peter waited for him to ring, for him to come home, but he never returned. Over thirty years later, they're still waiting.

Peter Boxell said recently that he's getting on in years, and doesn't 'want my life to end without discovering what happened to my son'. He and his wife are especially lovely people, and for their sakes as well as for Lee's sister, Lindsey, I want to try to progress this case as far as I can.

To begin with, the police treated it as a missing persons case, but I really don't think that Lee left home voluntarily. Notwithstanding the good relationship he had with his family, he left his bank card behind. With over £750 in his account, a large amount for a boy his age in 1988, Lee would not have gone very far for very long without taking that card with him.

In my opinion, the police could have handled the

initial investigation better, and it was the work done by the National Missing Persons Helpline (now known as the charity Missing People) and their investigators that made it clear something had happened to Lee and that it was likely he returned home to Cheam from Sutton that Saturday afternoon. (I have a longstanding relationship with the helpline, the two amazing sisters who established it – Janet Newman OBE and Mary Asprey OBE – and their dedicated staff. I was a police officer when the charity was first set up and worked with them from the outset, helping them establish links with forces around the country. Since then, they've provided assistance to me in many of my investigations.)

Standing in the centre of Cheam is St Dunstan's Church, a Victorian building. The site also houses a chapel that has stood there, in one form or another, for over 900 years. It's quite special, housing the monuments and brasses from the building that were placed inside the chapel from the fifteenth to the seventeenth centuries. Surrounding the church is a graveyard, and in a quiet corner is a modern structure that has replaced the small, somewhat run-down original brick building.

This building is where, during the eighties and nineties, gravedigger William Lambert ran an unofficial youth group known as 'the Shed'. Lee was recognized by visitors to the Shed as someone they'd seen there.

In 1988, Patrick James Lambert (William wasn't his given name) was in his mid-fifties and well known to the police. He had been first convicted of sex offences in the late 1960s, and convictions for other crimes, such as theft, dated back to the early 1950s. Somehow, though, Lambert was able to run this youth group with no one asking the right questions; another example of how paedophiles in the seventies and eighties could act with impunity if they embedded themselves in the right community.

The Shed was an informal gathering place. All kinds of teenagers would show up there, with no parental involvement or oversight; it's exactly the sort of place that would provide the perfect opportunities for a paedophile like Lambert. First of all, he would have chosen his victim carefully; his preferred target would be someone who, for whatever reason, didn't want to spend time at home. It could have been because their home life was chaotic as a result of alcohol or substance abuse, or because their parents were divorcing – there could have been a multitude of reasons.

I'm sure Lambert would have stoked up the sugges-tion that they were misunderstood by their parents, that he knew what their lives were like – how con-strained and unhappy they must feel at home – and would have made sure they knew he was prepared to let them do what they wanted at the Shed, in a way their parents would never have allowed them. He'd have told them how he appreciated them and their desires, and that he would overlook their mistakes as they experimented. He'd have spouted all sorts of manipulative rubbish that paedophiles like him do so as to gain the trust and lower the defences of those they've targeted.

All the unsolved cases from the seventies, eighties and nineties that I've mentioned before have never been added up properly. I've seen a figure of 1,500 quoted, but that only covers those recorded as murder cases; there are many more listed as missing persons. I believe the figure's too low, and that many of the missing persons cases are actually murders.

Missing children aren't always missing because they've been abducted. Over 180,000 people go missing every year, over half of them adults; most are found within twenty-four hours, but some disappear for ever. There's no doubt in my mind that Lee Boxell's case was, at the outset, mishandled, but thankfully both procedures and attitudes have changed considerably since then. Someone going to the police about their missing child in this day and age would not find themselves in the same situation as the Boxells did.

There is nearly always going to be an element of publicity around a missing persons case, because the police usually want to get the public's help as quickly as they can. Understandably, some families shy away from that. However, there are some stories that don't seem to suit the media's agenda as well as others: a child with drug-addiction problems, for instance, or the daughter of a single parent, isn't going to fit the narrative of some newspapers as well as a pretty young girl at the heart of a loving family. This is why stories such as those of Milly Dowler are far more readily spread across the front pages of the papers for the public to read than those of, say, Hannah Williams.

Milly Dowler went missing from Walton-upon-Thames in early 2002 and her remains were found twenty-five miles away in September that year. In 2011, Levi Bellfield, already serving a life sentence for murder, was convicted of Milly's murder and given an additional whole life tariff. The coverage of Milly's disappearance, and the search for her before her remains were discovered, dominated the news for months.

By way of contrast, Hannah Williams went missing from south-east London in April 2001 and her remains were discovered by chance about the same time Milly Dowler was abducted by Bellfield. Why is it that most of the country knew about Milly Dowler, but almost no one had heard about Hannah Williams's disappearance and lonely death?

This is not an attack on Milly's case; this is about the media, what kind of stories they claim appeal to their readership, and who they can use as a focus for the investigation to appeal to the public. The police described Hannah's mother, a single parent, as 'not really press-conference material'; Hannah had run away from home before, and the suggestion that her home life was complicated must have been enough for the papers to stay away from the story. Hannah's mother tried to find her daughter herself, putting up hundreds of posters in shops across south-east London; she was convinced her daughter hadn't simply run off, but had been abducted.

The following year, convicted sex offender Robert Howard was sentenced to life imprisonment for Hannah's murder. It turned out that he knew her; Howard's partner, oblivious to his true nature and past convictions, was Hannah's father's ex-girlfriend. Howard used his partner's phone to lure Hannah to meet him, before he raped and murdered her. He died in prison in 2015, a long history of rape charges and other violent crimes – including the suggestion that he had killed before, both in the UK and in Ireland – behind him.

Sadly, it still remains the case that although abduction by strangers occurs, it's the threat from someone who knows you or has met you – even if they seemed forgettable – that is the strongest. It's not just true of what happened to Hannah Williams; a more widely known case is that of missing girl Danielle Jones, who disappeared in June 2001. Her body has never been found. In fact, when Hannah's body was first discovered, it was initially believed to be Danielle's – it was only when the girl's distinctive clothing was shown to Hannah's mother that the remains were correctly identified.

Like Hannah, Danielle had been taken by someone who knew her – in this case her uncle, Stuart Campbell. Although her body has never been found, forensic work on both their mobile phones showed that Campbell had fabricated messages sent from her phone to pretend she was alive. Evidence found hidden in his house – a lipstick and some bloodstained stockings – also linked Campbell directly to Danielle. Once his alibi was disproved, his own diary, detailing his obsession with teenage girls and admitting to abuse he had carried out, provided the final pieces of damning evidence against him.

Both girls' murders are horrific, and for both families the aftershocks will never stop. However, Danielle Jones's case involved a BBC *Crimewatch* reconstruction and over 900 officers. The contrast with Hannah Williams's disappearance couldn't be more stark.

There are so many similar stories: young girls – and boys – taken off the streets, believed to have run away when in fact they've been forcibly abducted. A police officer involved in investigations into child abduction in Scotland told a reporter, 'There are lots of children who go missing but there is no publicity. Kids from poor families living on schemes, who roam the streets at night and have nobody who gives a damn, don't get the high-profile treatment.'

A 2002 article in the *Guardian* put it especially succinctly: 'There are certain rules in the missing persons game. Don't be a boy, don't be working class, don't be black. As for persistent runaways, children in care or teenagers with drug problems – forget it.'

In Lee Boxell's case, his disappearance happened during an era when young children went missing and the Metropolitan Police failed to get to grips with the case. When you have the staff of the National Missing Persons Helpline carrying out the investigation, going to ask questions of people who they think will be able to tell them something about Lee's disappearance, that's a sure sign that even though Lee was missing, the police were doing very little. They finally got hold of the investigation properly in April 2012, when a review was undertaken, but prior to that they had seemed to let it drift; and by then it was possibly too late to get all the answers for Lee's parents.

At the time of Lee's disappearance, William Lambert wasn't questioned by the police, despite being on the sex offenders register. Two years later, as part of the investigation, another man was overheard boasting about how he and some other young men had killed a boy and buried him in a tomb in the churchyard. After being questioned by police he was ruled out of the inquiry. His boasting had been exactly that, and nothing more.

Over the next several years, the investigation didn't really move forward. Lambert was questioned a number of times – in 1994 he was tried at the Old Bailey for raping teenage girls at the Shed, but acquitted and allowed to go back to work in the churchyard. The abuse would have continued. Finally, in 2011 he was convicted of raping and sexually assaulting four girls aged between eleven and fifteen at the club between 1985 and 1990. He was sentenced to serve eleven years.

Long before he was convicted, the police had started to probe Lambert's connections with Lee Boxell a little more closely. When interviewed in 1999, Lambert had admitted to knowing Lee, and claimed that Lee had a girlfriend his mother didn't approve of. This, he suggested, was why Lee had left home. This was hardly likely to be true, but Lambert's lies are in keeping with the paedophile's efforts to appear to 'know' children better than their parents, to be the keeper of their secrets and the only person they would truly confide in. Whether it's a technique they use to groom new targets, or something they tell themselves to pretend they are something they're not, I don't know. It certainly doesn't wash with what is known about Lee.

Throughout the investigation it seems Lambert carried on telling unlikely stories, suggesting that Lee had reappeared in Cheam once or twice over the years following his disappearance, to see 'the old haunts', but was now living under a new name in a nearby borough, working for the council. Lambert's version of events included new details, such as Lee supposedly being married and with a child of his own. In the wake of Lee's disappearance, pinned to the wall of the Shed was his 'missing' poster.

Different witnesses alleged that Lambert would use threats relating to Lee's disappearance to coerce them. It could have just been talk on his part, his intention being to terrify them into submission. While speaking to the authorities, Lambert suggested that if someone was murdered, one way to bury a body would be to do what the Kray twins had been rumoured to do with their dead enemies. That is, bury them in a graveyard below a coffin already there. To other visitors to the Shed, Lambert would also talk of the tunnels that had been built under the churchyard during the Second World War. He also mentioned that a body had been buried in a shallow grave in a local park.

None of Lambert's stories necessarily mean he had anything to do with Lee's disappearance. The activities in the Shed for which he was convicted gave him reason enough to be evasive with anyone looking into what was going on there around that time. But I'm convinced Lambert knows more about Lee's disappearance than he has previously let on. It's been suggested that on the day he vanished, rather than go to the football, Lee could have returned to Cheam for some reason and gone to visit the Shed. Why he was going there, if indeed that's where he was going, and whether or not he expected other teenagers to be there, we'll never know. It seems plausible that he stumbled on something he shouldn't have, or he refused to keep quiet about whatever it was he saw. One witness, going into the Shed alone one afternoon in late 1988, remembers there being a strong unpleasant smell in there and seeing a mattress heavily stained with blood – though she does admit that it was dark, and could only be sure that there was a large stain on the mattress.

When the police reopened the case in 2013, they interviewed Lambert in prison but he denied all knowledge of Lee being at the Shed that day. If something happened to Lee at the Shed, then I think two other men who knew Lambert well either were there and knew about it, or were later involved in some way. I've already traced the family of one of them and expect to speak to him soon.

I recently went back to Cheam and took a walk around the graveyard. Lee's body could well be in there – it's a big area, and there are lots of existing graves to have buried someone in. Many of the plots are especially old, and some have given way and sunk into the ground over time. In 2013, a year-long police operation took place during which the churchyard was excavated in the hope of finding new evidence that would shed light on Lee's case. Lee's body wasn't recovered, nor were any new pieces of evidence. They weren't permitted, though, to disturb any burial sites out of respect for the dead – they examined just under the surface of the graves to see if there had been any disturbance. So is it possible that a body might be concealed deeper than that, below an existing coffin?

There is also some fresh information that has come to light that might have a bearing on the investigation. A Swatch watch, identical to one owned by Lee (although it was a fairly common watch to have at the time, it was exactly the same model as his), was found right by the churchyard. This information is not yet in the public domain.

I wrote to the Prisoner Location Service and they told me that Lambert is not currently in prison, which means he has been released following his conviction in 2011. I've been trying to track him down, although there are all sorts of rumours being put about that I think are smokescreens to cover his whereabouts. He'd be approaching eighty-three years old, and perhaps at that age he might finally be prepared to tell the truth. I am determined to find Lambert and put my evidence to him.

Lee's case does tell us something about the way investigations into missing people – missing children, particularly boys – are handled. When Christine Boxell was trying to keep her son's story in the public eye – so as to maintain pressure on the police to continue investigating it, and possibly to prompt a witness to come forward – she would speak to the editors of newspapers to try to get Lee's name in the paper. One editor told her that they wouldn't run anything because he's 'just a fifteen-year-old boy'. 'That was tough to hear,' Christine told me. She feels that if her missing child had been a girl, things might have been different.

What must it be like for those parents whose child has never come home, and who never receives that level of public interest and determination to see a successful outcome in the shape of a returning loved one – such as Matthew Green, who I write about in Chapter 8 – or the successful prosecution of the person behind that adolescent's disappearance? What happens to the families, devastated by the unexpected disappearance of their daughter or son, who also have to face public as well as official indifference as the years go by?

8

ANOTHER STATISTIC

In the disappearance of Sarah Benford, offi-cers undertook over 5,000 lines of enquiry and compiled nearly 1,000 reports, but it still remains a major unsolved case on Northamptonshire Police's books and an example of devastating official indifference.

Sarah, aged fourteen, went missing from Welford House children's home in Northampton in April 2000. The residential home was a small one, looking after no more than a handful of children and supporting them in living away from their family homes. Sarah had moved there from her mother Vicki's terraced house in the north-east of Kettering, which she shared with her two siblings and their father, Sarah's stepfather, because of the people she had started to associate with – petty criminals and drug addicts near the family home.

Sarah had started stealing, egged on by these people, no doubt in the belief that she was helping them, her 'friends'. She'd go out to meet them, then a day or two later, she'd be caught and returned to Vicki by the police. This developed into a regular pattern of behaviour until Vicki involved the local social services. The idea of putting her daughter into care far away from home was to separate Sarah from these bad influences; Welford House was over fifteen miles away from the family's house in Kettering, and Vicki thought that being away from the area would help her troubled daughter.

Just because she was in care didn't mean that Sarah never saw her family, and she was in regular touch with Vicki. Vicki was aware that her daughter had started drinking, but was shocked to discover she was also taking heroin when Sarah appeared one day, 6 April, outside Vicki's work. Sarah told her mother that she was particularly unhappy in the children's home, had left it three days before, and wasn't planning to go back.

When she left that day, it was the last time Vicki ever saw her daughter.

I've written before that of the 180,000 people who go missing every year, over 80,000 of them are children. It's such a shocking statistic that it bears repeating, but for a child like Sarah, one in care, then the chances of becoming one of those missing children is far higher than if she were in a stable family home. One in every ten children looked after by social services goes missing, compared to one in every 200 of all children. Most are found quickly: 80 per cent within twenty-four hours; 90 per cent within two days. However, over 1,600 children every year, 2 per cent of the total, remain absent for longer than a week.

The statistics go on – the number of those who make contact either with a charity, social services or their families; the number who turn to crime; the number who are killed; and, saddest of all, the number who are never found. The statistics can tell one story but it is when you meet someone affected by such a tragedy – Sarah's mum, Vicki, for instance – that you fully begin to comprehend what it is like to live as one of these statistics.

Not all missing persons stories end unhappily; some have an unexpectedly positive outcome. In April 2010, Matthew Green, a roofer in his mid-twenties, from Sittingbourne in Kent, vanished one day. He had some history of mental illness, and was living with his parents. Pauline and Jim Green thought that everything was OK with Matthew when he told them he was going up to London to see a friend for the weekend. He never came back.

Matthew's parents were unable to establish if he'd even been to London, and as Sittingbourne is less than thirty-five miles from the port of Dover, it's possible that Matthew could have gone anywhere.

There were sightings of Matthew in the years that followed; someone said they'd seen him in Auckland in New Zealand, but it quickly became clear from the CCTV that this was a misidentification. Each time his birthday and Christmas came around, Pauline and Jim would buy their son presents and place them carefully in his bedroom, waiting for news.

The police, by the time I became involved three years after Matthew went missing, were pretty sure that he was dead. I thought he was alive, though. He'd been researching going to Australia to work, and I thought there was a possibility he'd gone there. Or at least had tried to get there. I covered his story for an ITV special on missing people, *Missing*, interviewing school friends, and others, but nothing came of the exposure – no one contacted us with evidence of any credible sightings of Matthew.

For six years, Pauline and Jim Green heard nothing, until one day, out of the blue, they were contacted by the UK police. Matthew was in a psychiatric hospital in Spain.

His parents couldn't quite believe what they were hearing. The snag was, Matthew hadn't given his permission to pass on his details to anyone – the police cited data protection laws – and so his parents couldn't even find out which hospital Matthew was in, let alone which city in which part of Spain. The Spanish authorities said they were duty-bound to honour the request of an adult in these circumstances, and I suppose that was right. This was Matthew's own family, though, and after six years of worry for them, it was cruel to know that he was safe but still out of reach.

I told Pauline I'd try to help. I covered the story of Matthew's discovery for ITV's *This Morning* and on BBC Radio 5 Live, and this media work prompted the Spanish hospital in Madrid to contact Pauline and Jim Green. They were able to confirm that Matthew was in their care, that he still didn't want to see his parents, but that the doctors treating him wanted as much background information on his mental health as Pauline and Jim could give them. He'd been living at the airport, apparently, and was severely unwell.

Having got this far, it was impossible not to take the next step. Having spoken to the consultant at the hospital myself, I flew to Spain with Pauline and Jim. The doctor said that we should come over, by all means, but he couldn't guarantee that Matthew would see any of us. So it proved. When we arrived, Matthew refused to see his parents, which devastated them further.

I couldn't sit and watch them suffer like that without trying to do something, so I asked them if they were prepared to go along with what I'd decided to do to try to get past this blockage.

'It might just help to get you in to see Matthew,' I told them.

Naturally they agreed – anything at that moment would have felt like a lifeline to them. We had to somehow engineer that first reconciliation between them so that they could all move forward – Matthew included.

I went to talk to the doctors.

'How about if I go in on my own to see him? I'm an old family friend,' I fibbed.

The consultant relented and I went in to meet Matthew, and explained who I really was. We spoke for about fifteen minutes, and I told him that his mum and dad had never given up hoping they'd find him again, that they cared about him deeply, and that they had some clothes and a bit of money for him.

He had nothing of his own to wear, so I said, 'Why don't we get them in to give you the clothes? You don't have to say anything to them, but they can hand them over.'

He agreed. Pauline and Jim came in and were able to give him the clothes they'd brought with them. Pauline also had a photograph of her grandson with her – Matthew's nephew, who he hadn't seen in the years since the child was a baby, and who had grown into a lovely young boy. We left the room after just four or five minutes, but Pauline said to me that the moment Matthew looked at the picture, it was confirmation for her that she'd got her son back.

The family, with help from me, then made efforts to get Matthew moved back to the UK. Sure enough, in less than a couple of months he was transferred to a UK hospital. He's still not fully able to come home – he isn't willing to be there full time – but it's great to know that someone written off by the police, with only the family themselves believing that one day he would be found, could be reunited with those who love him, even after such a long time.

It also goes to show that sometimes you have to push a little or bend the truth slightly to get the result you need. For Matthew's parents to be able to see their son finally when he was only a room or two away but behind closed doors, getting them in there was a direct result of my going that extra yard. When you work with people in the right way, and are confident in pushing boundaries with officialdom, you can get a positive result.

Not everyone is as lucky as the Green family. Sometimes those who go missing stay missing. Following her daughter Sarah's disappearance, Vicki searched all over Kettering for her. She would visit the parks she knew her daughter hung out in, she went to pubs, she spoke to anyone who she thought might know what had happened to her. She tried to get users on Kettering's drug scene to speak to her; sometimes she even got into fights with people if she thought they were being rude about Sarah.

After many years of waiting, hoping that her daughter would come back to her, Vicki became convinced that Kettering's drug community knew what had happened. In her eyes she thinks it's likely that the young, inexperienced girl took an accidental overdose and died, and that her death has been covered up by those people for fear of the effect it would have on all of them.

Vicki and her family were disappointed by the initial reaction of the police. Perhaps, just like the case of Hannah Williams, it's unsurprising that there was little official action in the early days of Sarah's absence. Here was a girl who had gone missing before, and who had started hanging out with a crowd whose main aim in life was to stay outside the law.

The police didn't launch a murder investigation until three years later. In June 2003, the police searched two homes in Kettering and one nearly 200 miles away, near Port Talbot in South Wales. More searches in and around the Kettering area took place over the following months, but then the investigation petered out. Over a decade later, in March 2016, the police searched a wooded area near Kettering that they had been led to believe might harbour the remains of Sarah's body, but nothing related to her was found. (The search did unearth a gun, however, so it wasn't entirely fruitless.) To date, eight people have been arrested in connection with her murder, but they've all been released. The police now say that they believe Sarah died, as Vicki also does, from an accidental overdose in the first few days after she went missing. Her body has never been found and no one has ever been charged with any crime in relation to her disappearance.

One newspaper reported, 'It is also believed she became addicted to heroin and may have worked as a prostitute to fund her habit.' Words such as these don't infuriate me, but I think we need to consider our language more carefully. I don't believe in the use of the term 'child prostitution'; if the victim is a child, and someone has sex with that child knowing he or she is a child, then that is child abuse. It doesn't matter whether the victim is paid or not.

If someone is grooming a child, giving them gifts and then having sex with them, that isn't considered having sex with a prostitute, that is abuse. Why, then, is it any different when that 'gift' turns out to be addictive drugs, and the child knows that the only way they can pay for those drugs is by having sex with adults? The phrase 'child prostitution' is a cover for abuse – that's it.

A friend of Sarah's family asked for my help in the summer of 2017, seventeen years after she disappeared, and I've carefully assessed the case, reading the file and looking closely at what is known about the drug world in the area. Vicki Benford said that she took action to get Sarah taken into Welford House to prevent her from being drawn further into a network of criminality, stealing for drug addicts and petty criminals. However, she knows now that this was never going to stop Sarah, and that the protection she hoped Sarah would receive in the home wasn't sufficient to prevent what eventually happened. I was shown a document from the care home which spelled out that Sarah was having sex, using drugs and self-harming with knives, all in the weeks before she finally walked out the door and disappeared for ever.

I also saw some up-to-date reports about the drug situation in Kettering, which recorded multiple incidents in the area where Sarah had lived with her mother. One such report was about a fourteen-year-old girl who'd been arrested for possession with intent to supply class A drugs; she'd hidden the drugs in her underwear. It seemed that little has changed since Sarah went missing.

Vicki's assumption that Sarah died from an accidental overdose is possible, and information I have to consider, but I also have to assess the possibility that something far more unpleasant happened: for years, known paedophiles and child abusers have operated across the care home system in the UK. There have been substantial investigations into claims of historic child abuse in care homes, and many of those investigations are ongoing.

I've addressed some of the issues relating to claims of historic child abuse in connection with the Jimmy Savile case (see Chapter 6). But for Sarah's investigation I need to find out which known offenders, if any, were operating in the areas she frequented, and if the timelines overlapped. It might be that the offender was unknown to the police at that time, but I had to begin with material my team and I could research readily.

In December 2017, along with Specialist Group International (SGI), an acknowledged expert search organization run by my good friend Peter Faulding (I work with SGI regularly), I searched a house in Kettering which we were told by a witness was one of the last places Sarah had been seen alive. We took with us a full forensic team, including a specialist search outfit who brought a bank of equipment with them. One particular piece of kit was ground-penetrating radar, which would help to target areas in and around the ground floor of the house and garden that we should explore further.

We excavated the whole of the back yard, but didn't find anything. The ground-penetrating radar, however, showed an anomaly below the surface. Once several scans had been collated, a cavity was revealed in the ground beneath a thick concrete path. The space was big enough to hold a human body, so we decided to break up the concrete and investigate.

The owner said the police had searched the house in previous years. They too had used ground-penetrating radar but had told the owner they would have to come back another time as they didn't have the resources that would allow them to break up the concrete, dig through the soil and replace it all once they'd finished. They never did come back, but I'm glad we were able to complete the job for them, as the owner told us that she was concerned that there might have been a body buried there.

The dig revealed no body but instead a well, which rather surprised the owner, who had no idea such a thing was there.

Despite not finding anything in our search, a positive result did come from the action we'd taken. Knowing that we were intent on trying to find Sarah's body meant that some people who'd been reluctant to speak to us beforehand, perhaps thinking we weren't that serious about finding out the truth about Sarah's disappearance, now felt able to speak to us.

A friend of Sarah's contacted me. We knew already that Sarah had been drinking alcohol during her last few weeks at the children's home, but this friend told us that while we might think we knew that Sarah had also been taking drugs, we didn't know when it had first started, how frequently it had been happening – or, indeed, who had introduced Sarah to drugs in the first place. We *did* already know how Sarah, aged only fourteen, was able to obtain them, but this friend confirmed our suspicions.

Sarah had been lured into a world in which she had no chance of survival. As an immature young girl, she and a small group of girls around her age were being exploited by a group of older men, who no doubt were telling Sarah and the others that they were 'their friends'. Those 'friends' were making drugs available, and this was the key to forcing the young girls to do their bidding.

These exact methods were being used by the grooming gangs later prosecuted in Rotherham, Rochdale and elsewhere. As more evidence about their activities comes out, the picture in cases such as Sarah Benford's becomes sharper and clearer. The abusers prey on girls in care homes, vulnerable and ripe for exploitation as they are. The men befriend these children, and use drugs to either ensure the compliance of the unfortunate girls or simply to allow the abusers to force themselves upon their victims. In the case of the latter, the chances of something violent happening are hugely increased.

The use of the word 'gangs' when discussing these appalling cases can be a bit misleading. This is no *Godfather*-style Mafia, with rules and hierarchies and meetings. These groups consisted of like-minded men who would locate and groom girls for themselves and for others in their circle who would carry out the same awful acts as them.

Perhaps the most notorious case of a girl abducted and abused by gangs such as this is that of Charlene Downes, killed in Blackpool in 2003. She was fourteen years old. Police and other organizations have said there were particularly high levels of child sexual abuse in Blackpool around that time, with young girls being targeted by men working in the fast-food businesses that filled the back streets and alleyways of Blackpool.

It's believed that the girls, some younger than Charlene, were offered cigarettes and free food by those men in exchange for sex. What happened to Charlene has never been determined; her body has never been found. There were grim rumours that some of the men involved in abusing her had laughingly suggested she'd been cut up and put into kebabs in the fast-food outlets they either worked in or owned, but that horrendous allegation has never been proved.

Loosely organized paedophile gangs are not restricted to northern England either. In south-west London, Levi Bellfield, who was already serving three life sentences for murder when he was convicted of the killing of Milly Dowler (see Chapter 7), is believed to have operated with other men who would have non-consensual sex with underage girls; the men would drug these children before they had sex with them, or rape other girls. They would also film the attacks and circulate the videos within the group; the girls were often dressed in school uniform before the men assaulted them.

The men into whose orbit Sarah Benford had travelled were known to include in their midst at least one adult pornographer who liked to take photographs and make videos of young girls as well. Sarah's friend was able to give me his name, and also told me she had seen Sarah at this man's bedsit above a video shop, which may or may not have been a studio for filming rather than the place he actually lived, and that Sarah had been there with a man she described as 'Chinese'. She was sure that Sarah had fallen in with this bad lot and had ended up being killed by them, or by someone connected to them. The contact gave me a whole list of names, in addition to the pornographer's, which I've now passed to the police.

Not all of the names were people I believe abused Sarah and the other girls. At least one is another girl who, I'm told, had an argument with Sarah and may well be able to tell me more about what was going on at the time. The more information I can find out about the last few months of Sarah's life, the better; it will help build up a case for the police if they are ever in a position to charge someone with Sarah's murder, and it will help Vicki understand a little more of what was going on in her daughter's chaotic existence at that time. It won't bring her any comfort, but it might bring some understanding.

I've also been told that some individuals in the social services department who dealt with Sarah's case were aware of the sort of group she was on the periphery of; that they knew the type of people circling around the care homes in the area, singling out potential victims. These social workers were told to stay away and not to get involved; which is reminiscent of the way in which authorities turned a blind eye to some of the abuse going on in Rochdale, and other places across England, that has recently been uncovered. I'll also need to find out more about this allegation; after Savile, I've grown tired of hearing the excuse 'We didn't know', when it was clear that the authorities did, and did nothing about it.

I'm always aware of the impact any investigation I carry out has on the people involved, on the families. Jessie Earl's parents (see Chapter 9) told me that they were really pleased with where we had got to in the investigation into Jessie's death, but that they had felt the strain of being back on the emotional merry-go-round, going round and round again, every day. Their anguish had receded somewhat; they'd put it to bed in the years following her disappearance. Of course it came up every now and again, but as we moved forward with our investigation, they were having to live through the emotional trauma of missing their daughter over and over again. I made sure they knew that I understood – it must be so hard to deal with the upset when you think you've got it under control but then outside events bring all those dormant feelings back to the surface again.

It's easy to underestimate what emotional reactions are provoked by investigators, and journalists, when we go in to cover a story but get to come out again and carry on with our lives. We meet victims' families at the worst possible time, and what we leave behind is torment. Police officers also meet with families at critical and traumatic times. Then, as soon as a successful prosecution has taken place and someone's gone to jail, or an investigation peters into nothing, they are off again; although family liaison officers will often remain in contact for years after an event.

I try to stay in touch with people I've worked with over the years. I say to them, 'You've got my number. If there's any time I can help you, just ring me.' Look at Matthew Green's case – I'd worked with the family until there seemed to be nothing left to do, and nowhere for the investigation to go, but then Pauline Green got in touch again as soon as they heard the news that Matthew was alive. I was delighted to get that call, and I'd like to think that everyone I've worked with since I left the police knows that I am there for them if they need to speak to me, so I make sure they know my phone number remains open to them for the rest of my life.

I've seen what happens over the years to the parents, the brothers and sisters of loved ones whose whereabouts remain unknown. They carry on, because they have to. Then either they become totally consumed by their feelings – hatred, anger, guilt, you name it – and curl up and die because that level of negativity finishes them off; or they learn how to manage their feelings on a day-to-day basis and allow their rage to dissipate as they try to carry on with their lives.

The people I feel most strongly for are those such as Louise Kay's mum, who died without finding out what happened to her daughter. To die not knowing the truth, not knowing where your child is, or what end they met, must be beyond devastating. The loss of a child is surely one of the toughest things to handle – it's difficult enough simply to contemplate; but for that child to die in circumstances where you don't have the answers adds another level of gut-piercing emotional pain.

All of us – or at least the vast majority of us – want to believe that there is good in people, but we also want to believe that when there isn't, then justice will prevail. Sadly, it doesn't – not always. There are families out there who will never get the justice they seek.

Now, nearly twenty years after Sarah's disappearance, I'm still pursuing that justice for Sarah, and for Vicki. My investigation has convinced me that she was murdered very soon after going missing; the police, I know, believe this too. Vicki has also come around to this way of thinking, although she hoped for longer than the professionals that her daughter would resurface eventually and make contact with her again.

The victims of the Rochdale and Rotherham grooming gangs saw justice when the men who had abused them – or, at least, many of the ringleaders – were sent to jail, most of them for lengthy terms. The details of the crimes are appalling so perhaps even these sentences aren't enough, but at least the local communities became aware of what was happening in their midst and were able to see how vulnerable people – children in care – were being exploited. Lessons were learned by the authorities about managing the safety of vulnerable individuals so maybe cases such as these, and Sarah Benford's, will become increasingly rare as we no longer treat children in care, especially girls, as third-class citizens.

I'm certain that Sarah Benford found herself caught up in an organized child abuse network and paedophile ring that was taking young people from children's homes in the Midlands, just as the ones operating in Yorkshire were. These children were run by pimps, fed drugs and forced by adults to take part in sexual activity that was filmed. What happened to Sarah in that mix is what I need to confirm. I'm hoping in time to be in a position to expose the real reason for Sarah's murder, to identify the key suspect, and to provide the police with enough evidence to charge him.

I hope for the chance to find out if I can get a result of the same magnitude in a case that I originally took on in 2017: two young women who had gone missing several decades earlier, Louise Kay and Jessie Earl.

9

VICTIMS OF
A SERIAL KILLER?

LOUISE KAY AND JESSIE EARL BOTH WENT MISSING
on the south coast of England, Louise in June 1988
and Jessie in May 1980. Louise was only eighteen.
After a night out in Eastbourne, she and her car vanished, never to be seen again. Jessie, four years older,
had also gone missing in Eastbourne and remained so
until her skeletal remains were found about five miles
away, above Beachy Head, in 1989.

Initially, I was only investigating the disappearance
of Louise Kay, but it soon became clear that the two
cases were linked.

One of the key elements of the investigation into
Louise's disappearance was the whereabouts of her
car, a distinctive gold Ford Fiesta, with the driver's
door painted white. It would be a lot harder to dispose of such a vehicle than a young girl's body. If that
makes me sound like I'm being too bleak, I'd point

out that if she moved away to start a new life – ran off abroad, or something like that – she would have left her car behind.

So I believe she was taken and killed and her body buried somewhere. That itself makes her particularly hard to find – but what would have happened to her car?

Louise's mother spent twenty years searching for answers, before she herself died. She had kept excellent records of all the efforts she'd made, speaking to people, following up any kind of lead she could that might reveal what had happened to Louise. One of those notes, taken from conversations with Louise's friends about the time she vanished, suggested that Louise had been given money for petrol by 'a Scottish man'.

This brief reference rang a particularly strong alarm bell for me.

There was known to be 'a Scottish man', who had since been jailed for killing young women, living on the south coast of England at that time. He had been apprehended after murdering a young woman in Scotland, and his name was Peter Tobin.

Following his arrest in 2006 for the rape and murder of Angelika Kluk in Glasgow, police searched the garden of Peter Tobin's former home in Margate, where they found two more bodies: Vicky Hamilton and Dinah McNicol. Both had been killed in 1991;

Vicky disappeared from Scotland, and Dinah from Hampshire. Margate is only eighty miles away from Eastbourne, and police had information that, around the time Louise Kay disappeared, Tobin was working at a small hotel in Eastbourne. He was also known, according to the police in Scotland who investigated the crimes he was believed to have committed, to be trying to sell a small, hand-painted car. (I tried to corroborate this report, but could find no record of a car being repainted, retaxed, sold or scrapped.)

Whatever had happened to Louise's gold car, one thing was certain: it had simply vanished. Tobin dealt in cars; he was paid to deliver them around the country for an auction company. He would be a familiar face at many garages across the UK and, more importantly, he would also have had access to scrapyards. Travelling around as much as he did, staying in places for a short space of time and using multiple aliases, made tracing Tobin's movements especially difficult for the police and, decades later, for me and my team.

We did what we could to piece together a picture of the kind of man Tobin was. His early life revealed a particularly disturbing past. In his early twenties, he stabbed the woman who later became his first wife, and married her in Brighton – far from Glasgow and, ironically, given what was to happen later on, close to Eastbourne. He married again, twice, but those wives too left him when he demonstrated his real personality.

In 1993, he attacked and raped two fourteen-year-old girls he had lured to his flat; after he had stabbed one of them, he left with his five-year-old son – who'd been in the flat while Tobin assaulted the two children – but not before turning on the gas taps, thinking he'd conceal evidence by burning down his own house. Tobin was eventually caught and in 1994 he was jailed for fourteen years, but released in 2004.

I looked into the disappearance of other young women in and around the area of Eastbourne during the early 1980s, to see what other links to Tobin I could find. I came across the story of Jessie Earl before very long.

Peter Tobin is a sexual opportunist who hid or buried his victims. Of all the awful, vile people I've had the misfortune to come across, Tobin is the worst, the least humane person I know. Since his arrest for murder, he will not give the families of his victims the answers they seek, he's refused to engage with the police, he does not care what they ask him, and he says nothing to help alleviate the suffering of families desperate for news of a missing daughter. It is up to my team and me to see what we can find that will help identify his involvement in the crimes we fear he might have committed; from our lists, and narrowing them down to those that fit his methodology as a killer, we've isolated over thirty cases to be looked into – including those of Louise Kay and Jessie Earl.

Louise Kay is buried somewhere Tobin had easy access to. His movements around the south coast are hard to track, but I managed to locate one address where Tobin was living at the time of Louise's disappearance, and which hasn't yet been searched by the police. It's in Brighton, but frustratingly I can't get permission from the owners – Brighton & Hove City Council – to get into the property, and more importantly the garden, to carry out a forensic search. They tell me the tenants have objected and, until the police demand a search, they see no reason to help us in our investigation. As yet, the police will not make an application to do so.

At the time Tobin lived at the Brighton address, the garden at the property was overlooked slightly less than the garden in Kent where Dinah and Vicky Hamilton's bodies were found. Consider that: fewer people could see into the Brighton garden than one where Tobin had buried two bodies. Anyone looking at that might say, there's no way he could have done it – but he did do it, not once but twice. It's amazing what people can get away with if they want to. And there's great privacy in the Brighton garden.

I was able to track down one former resident of the house, but any hopes I had that she would recall Tobin digging the garden (into which he could have put Louise Kay's body) were crushed when she could only remember that she didn't like him much, and that he kept himself to himself. However, she did confirm that he occupied the garden flat.

I don't know if Louise Kay's body is in that back garden, but I do know that line of enquiry can't be ignored. I'm sure her remains are buried on a property or in a piece of ground that Tobin could get to easily – that's how he got rid of his victims. Why won't the council – who are, after all, the owners of the building, rather than the tenants – give us permission to conduct a search? There would be no cost to them, and it would give some peace of mind to the Kay family, even if Louise wasn't found there.

Sussex Police have told me they couldn't connect Peter Tobin to the death of either Louise Kay or Jessie Earl, but I feel the alarming parallels between these two cases and Tobin's known offending patterns can't be ignored.

Jessie Earl's remains were found only a short walk from one of the car parks where Louise Kay used to park when she came to Beachy Head at night. At the time she went missing, Jessie's death was not treated as murder – the police took a deliberate policy decision to treat it as a missing persons case, and this has had ramifications through the years, and not just for Jessie's distraught family. I understand that no police officer, senior or otherwise, wants an unsolved murder on their books, and that Eastbourne is a beautiful place, but what was it that dictated the decision-making process of the police to call it a missing persons case?

When the remains of Jessie's naked body were eventually found in 1989, a crucial piece of evidence showed that her death couldn't be anything other than an unlawful killing. Jessie's bra was found near her remains, a knot in it tied so tightly that it could only have been used as a means of restraining her. Tobin's later victims had their hands tied behind their backs with their own underwear.

The coroner at the inquest into Jessie's death in 1989 recorded an open verdict, which has always rankled with Jessie's mother and father; they knew she hadn't run off but had been killed. This view was corroborated by the discovery of her remains, and the subsequent police investigation (begun in 2000) that treated her death as murder. The coroner has not responded to requests to review the original inquest verdict, but I am now working with David Wells, for free, to assist Jessie's parents in petitioning the High Court for a formal review; the initial stages of which have involved me making a submission to the Attorney General's office.

For Jessie's family, this is an incredibly important step and one that will ensure there is no confusion in anyone's mind as to what happened to their daughter. My respect for the Earls is off the scale; they have trusted the authorities time and again to get things right for Jessie. They've been let down repeatedly, but they keep on going, determined to see justice done for her. For me, as well as assisting them, it will enable me to start treating Jessie Earl as another potential victim of Peter Tobin; and perhaps bring more pressure to bear on the police to conduct a thorough search of the house in Brighton where he lived.

The idea that Tobin – known to have killed three women, and who was now under suspicion for murdering Jessie Earl and Louise Kay – had somehow carried out the attack on his first wife in 1970 and then done nothing more till he was convicted of attacking the two fourteen-year-olds in his own flat in 1993 seemed outlandish. I was sure there were other victims; someone with Tobin's proclivities doesn't just stop, and then start killing again many years later. My team and I started to look at cases of unsolved murders and missing people over an extended time period, covering Tobin's adult life, and focused on women and girls between the ages of fourteen and thirty-five.

The dead were to be found all over the UK, and it's my belief that a large number of those listed as 'missing' in the files are themselves dead, buried or somehow hidden from the reach of families, the police and those searching for them. It's certainly easier for a police force to list someone as 'missing' when there's no concrete evidence of a crime, but if there's no reason for someone to run away, if they take nothing they'd need with them – their money, their passport – then in our increasingly digital world it seems hard to imagine them living another life somewhere else.

Far more likely is that their bodies will be found one day, as Jessie Earl's was.

Jessie's remains were discovered by chance one afternoon when a man and his daughter were flying a kite on the hills above the English Channel at Beachy Head. The kite blew about on the high winds and dropped into some dense undergrowth. The father was all for abandoning the cheap toy, but his daughter insisted they recover it. He forced his way deep into the bushes and that's when he came across the skeletal remains of a person later confirmed to be Jessie Earl.

How many times had someone come close to finding her before? How many other bodies – or what is left of the bodies – lie out in the countryside, in heathland, woods, or on the edge of places where people walk, run and play regularly? I'm certain that there are many other victims out there, waiting to be dug up, waiting to be stumbled upon. It's one reason why I keep on looking, and keep on helping families such as the Earls. Because there are many other grieving loved ones out there, waiting for an answer.

As I've talked about previously, advances in forensic science have helped solve various old cases when DNA evidence has been recovered and then tested. Sadly, in Jessie's case, a crucial item of clothing, Jessie's own bra that had been used to restrain her, was not retained by the SIO involved. Because he decided to treat her disappearance as that of a missing person, there was no requirement to hold on to her clothing. Had that bra been kept (and if the case had been treated as a murder it would've been), the killer would likely have been caught.

The great strides forward in forensic science have made a huge difference to the investigations into cold-case crimes, and nowhere more so than in the ways DNA can be harvested. Provided the evidence from the crime scene was properly stored, DNA can be retrieved from the smallest amount of material and can provide a control against which samples taken from offenders can be tested, ruling them in – or out – as suspects.

In the past, when DNA evidence first started being used to solve cases, sample amounts had to be big enough to be visible – the size of a large coin. Now they can be incredibly small, no bigger than the dot from the tip of a pen. People who thought they got away with a crime decades ago unexpectedly find their past catching up with them, and families who never thought they'd see justice are finally able to get their day in court and watch the person who harmed their loved one go to jail.

The first time DNA evidence was used to secure a conviction was in 1986. Two fifteen-year-old girls had been killed in Leicestershire in the space of three years, and a local man had confessed to one murder – but not the other. DNA testing showed that he was innocent of both. The police asked all the men in the local area to give a DNA sample and drew a blank, until they were told by someone who'd overheard a conversation in a pub that local baker Colin Pitchfork had asked someone to give a sample on his behalf. Pitchfork was duly taken into custody; his DNA was tested and proven to be a match, and he was convicted of the two killings.

Developments in DNA sampling raced ahead in the 1990s and, in 2003, Craig Harman was convicted of dropping a brick off a motorway bridge into the window of a passing lorry and killing the driver. Harman, who had no previous arrests or convictions and had therefore never given a DNA sample, was caught because his brother's DNA *was* on the database and the police were able to link that partial match to Harman.

In 2009, a man who'd served twenty-seven years in jail was released when DNA evidence showed that he could not be a killer. Sean Hodgson was convicted of the murder of Teresa de Simone in Southampton in 1979, even though he had a proven history of confessing to crimes he did not commit. In fact, the crimes didn't even happen. He was extremely fortunate that swabs taken back in 1979 were still stored somewhere, because it was that evidence that led to the quashing of his conviction nearly three decades later. This goes to underline the value of retaining key evidence in an investigation even after a conviction has been secured. Not only was an innocent man freed from jail, but the DNA also enabled police to identify the real killer, who had committed suicide in 1988.

It has often been the case that a perpetrator of a major crime has been traced through the most innocuous of offences. Speeding offences have led, as in Brian Field's case, to murder convictions. The police have made it a point to take DNA swabs from anyone they breathalyse on the side of the road for drink-driving, for instance; and anyone arrested and charged with a recordable offence has to give a DNA sample. The database of samples now runs to well over five million people; and somewhere in there can be the clue needed to trace a criminal.

It doesn't always have to be the offender's own DNA that leads to their conviction. There have been a number of cases where a family member has had to give a sample – as in Craig Harman's case – which has then led to the arrest and conviction of a relative who has offended. Take James Lloyd, the rapist in South Yorkshire in the 1980s who collected his victims' shoes and was caught after his sister was breathalysed. Or the murder of Hannah Foster, who was killed in Southampton in 2003. Her killer, Maninder Pal Singh Kohli, fled to India. His wife and his brother – a police officer in India – declared him innocent, but the DNA traces left in his van, which provided a partial match to that given by his two young sons, told a different story. After Hannah's family tried for five years to get him extradited from India, Kohli was finally brought back to the UK in 2008 and sentenced to a minimum of twenty-four years in jail.

One of the best-known cases of how DNA profiling can secure a conviction is that of the murder of Colette Aram in Keyworth, Nottinghamshire, in 1983. Incidentally, the case was also the first one covered by BBC's *Crimewatch* when it started broadcasting in 1984. In 2008, a young man's DNA was taken after he was arrested on a motoring offence, and a database search showed a close match with samples taken from the victim's body in the 1983 murder. The young man was only twenty years old, so he could not be the killer; his father, Paul Hutchinson, however, was arrested and subsequently confessed to the crime. At the time of the initial investigation, Hutchinson had written anonymous letters to the police, taunting them and claiming, 'No one knows what I look like. That is why you have not got me. You will never get me.' Fateful words.

Here is not the place to debate the benefits and problems that would be associated with a national DNA database on which every adult in the country is registered. Many people have strong opinions for and against this idea, and I'm not going to devote pages and pages to discussing an issue which is covered in depth by many others, elsewhere. However, I'm always prepared to illustrate the value of the existing database, where criminals who have been registered on the system for relatively trivial offences in the past are then caught when they go on to commit more serious crimes.

Steve Wright had his DNA taken in 2002 when he stole £80 from the pub in which he worked. In 2006, five women in Ipswich were killed in a short space of time, and Wright was caught and convicted when DNA evidence showed he had had contact with three of the women; two of the victims' bodies had been deposited in water and the police believed he'd done this to prevent detection from DNA left on the bodies.

The media focused almost as much of their attention on the lifestyles of the five women, who were targeted by Wright as they were working as prostitutes, as they did on Wright. At one point during the initial investigation, the Assistant Chief Constable advised women to stay away from Ipswich's red light area. In my eyes, that's completely the wrong way to go about handling a police operation of this nature. It's victim-blaming, and my solution would be for police officers to act in such a way as not to criminalize these women, but to protect them. The offender is the criminal, not them. Police to the vulnerable, I call it. Resources should be aimed at those in society who most need protection and they should be provided with the same level of safety that is often given to the already secure in society.

However, there will always be predators who target the vulnerable. Single women, walking back in the dark, alone after a night out, or hitchhiking home; these are the images that people have of women who fall foul of attackers. It isn't always that way, of course; often a woman will be approached by someone who seems to be nothing but helpful, considerate and kind – before he reveals his true face. Peter Tobin was one such man.

Tobin was born in Scotland and it was in a Glasgow dance hall in 1968 that he met his wife-to-be, Margaret. Initially, he was 'quite the gentleman' but he soon turned and trapped her in his flat, raping her regularly, tormenting her with a knife which, one day, he used to stab her. He left her there and it was the downstairs neighbour, noticing blood coming through the ceiling, who called an ambulance. In hospital, Tobin reappeared, instructing Margaret not to say anything to the police before he led her – still injured – out of hospital and down to Brighton, over 460 miles away. There they married but she left him within a year, and is in no doubt that he was capable of going on to kill more than the three women he's been convicted of murdering. What did he do after he'd tried to kill her, she wonders: 'Once a murderer, always a murderer.'

With those words ringing in our ears, my investigative team and I redoubled our efforts to try to solve more of the cold-case crimes we had listed.

Three of the women on our list were killed in Glasgow in 1977. Over a period of four months, each of these three women – Anna Kenny, aged twenty; Hilda McAuley, aged thirty-six; and Agnes Cooney, aged twenty-three – went out for the evening and never returned home. At the time, the police felt that the manner in which the murders were committed – the abduction from the streets, the strangulations and sexual assaults, and how the bodies were left to be discovered in countryside or woodland – suggested that the perpetrator had carried out attacks like this before, and would do so again.

I thought that while there were many overlapping points of similarity with Peter Tobin's modus operandi, there were other variations, common to each of the three killings, that did not fit with what we knew Tobin did to the women he had already been convicted of killing. The way in which these women's bodies were tied, for instance, and the brazen way they were left to be discovered by passers-by; Tobin chose to hide his victims away by burying them.

However, there were other murders that bore a significant resemblance to these three unsolved Glasgow killings, and they also took place in Scotland – but on the coast, in Edinburgh. They were known as the notorious World's End killings and they happened in the same year – 1977 – when two young women, Christine Eadie and Helen Scott, both seventeen, left the World's End pub. Their bodies were found the next day, and the manner of their injuries, and the way the bodies had been treated and left in the open, was remarkably similar to the three Glasgow murders.

The killings of these two young women in Edinburgh were solved in 2014 when advances in forensic techniques allowed police to identify the murderer as Angus Sinclair; he was already in jail, serving time for the killing of a seventeen-year-old girl in Glasgow, Mary Gallacher, in 1978, when the forensic breakthrough came. However, if we thought this would be the route in to solving the three Glasgow cases, then that expectation was quickly rubbished; all the evidence in the cases of the three young women – Anna Kenny, Hilda McAuley and Agnes Cooney – had been destroyed, meaning there was nothing with any DNA on it. I'd have to do some old-fashioned policing – trawling through the files, speaking to witnesses, and checking everything in detail against what we could confirm about Angus Sinclair.

Sinclair was only sixteen years old when he killed eight-year-old Catherine Reehill in 1961, pushing her down the stairs of his tenement after raping her. A mere seven years later, when he was released from prison, Sinclair resumed his vile activities; he was eventually jailed in 1982, only this time not for murder, but for assault and rape, as he admitted multiple charges of raping females aged between six and fourteen years.

I believe he knew that if he admitted to these crimes, the police wouldn't look into his actions any further, and he was right; but my investigation showed that by 1982 he was responsible for the three murders – the World's End ones and Mary Gallacher – for which, in two separate trials, he was later convicted and imprisoned. As well as the four killings outlined above, I believe compelling evidence exists that shows at least one other unsolved murder can be attributed to Sinclair as the killer.

Sinclair was married and living in Edinburgh when Anna Kenny, Hilda McAuley and Agnes Cooney were all killed within four months of each other. His wife told me that around that time he spent every weekend driving to and from Glasgow, claiming that he was doing extra work painting and decorating to make some money.

He would travel in his white Toyota HiAce caravanette, which he told his wife they could use to holiday around Scotland. Although he kitted it out for their future trips, with curtains and a fold-out bed from the seats in the back, it was his main vehicle for getting to and from work. Accordingly, he kept his decorating tools, wires, screwdrivers, drills, rope and cable in the caravanette – and pairs of his wife's tights that she'd discarded. Both Anna Kenny and Hilda McAuley were found with their arms bound by torn tights.

Given that the caravanette was probably not only the repository for the tools that Sinclair used to carry out his crimes, but also the way in which he was able to entice young women into accepting a lift home, I sought to prove sightings of his distinctive vehicle in the areas where the murder victims were abducted and where their bodies were later discovered.

Anna Kenny's body was found, many months after she was killed, in a ditch on the Mull of Kintyre, well over a hundred miles away from Glasgow. The week-end she died, a local shepherd saw a vehicle resembling Sinclair's parked on the edge of a side road close to where the body was finally discovered. It stuck in his mind because the curtains in the vehicle were drawn even though it was, in his words, a 'lovely warm after-noon'. He was certain the sighting was that particular weekend because the date was fixed in his mind. He had, with his sheepdog, won a competition that week-end, and the date engraved on the trophy was the very weekend Anna Kenny disappeared.

Agnes Cooney was found twenty-three miles from Glasgow, shortly after she had vanished. The alcohol that would have been in her body – she'd been out drinking, seeing a band play in a pub, on the night she was abducted – had been metabolized by the time her body was found, which suggests she was kept alive for twenty-four hours before she was killed.

The caravanette would have been the ideal place to hold someone captive in secret. A witness saw a 'white van' in the vicinity where Agnes's body was dumped, on the same night; he described it as a Volkswagen caravanette, but recalled the beginning and the end of the number plate – 'RGG' and 'R', which he noted because it was similar to his father's plate. Sinclair's number plate was RGG 216R, and when I showed a photograph of the Toyota to the witness, he said without hesitation, 'That's the vehicle. I can be sure of that.'

The police never showed him that photograph. Worse, at the time, and following this witness's statement, the police issued an appeal for sightings of a Volkswagen caravanette, not a Toyota, and Sinclair was able to dispose of his van. The inside of the vehicle, its fixtures and fittings, the carpets, the seat covers, the curtains, all would have told their awful story through the recovery of DNA, there's no doubt about that – but everything was destroyed, never to be found.

On the night before Hilda McAuley's body was discovered, a witness parked in a lay-by near the area where Hilda was later found. She saw a man walk out of the darkness and up the lane right past her car. As it was dark, her car had its headlights on, which gave her a clear view of the man. I flew out to the Channel

Islands to interview her and, after I showed her a photograph of Sinclair – whom she'd never heard of before – she identified him as the man who'd walked past her car.

So I was able to place either Sinclair or his vehicle in three crucial areas – where each of the women's bodies were found. Added to this was the method of killing, which was identical to the ways in which the two World's End murders took place, and I think I can be certain in saying that Angus Sinclair was the killer of Anna Kenny, Hilda McAuley and Agnes Cooney. However, following Sinclair's death in March 2019, the police are highly unlikely to reopen the cases.

I also believe he carried out, with the aid of an accomplice, the June 1977 murder of thirty-seven-year-old Frances Barker. Thomas Ross Young died in prison serving a sentence for killing her, but claimed right up until the end that Sinclair was the murderer. Sinclair had had an accomplice before; his brother-in-law, Gordon Hamilton, was believed to have been involved in the World's End killings but had died some time ago.

At the initial trial for these two crimes, Sinclair sought to blame his late brother-in-law, saying that sex with Christine Eadie and Helen Scott had been consensual (he had to come up with some reason as to why his DNA was on the bra he'd taken off one of the victims to tie her up with), but that any harm done to women had been perpetrated by Hamilton. However, the jury considered the nature of the sexual activity with the two young women before they were killed to be clearly non-consensual and he was, at the second attempt, convicted.

There were definitely other offences committed by Sinclair, and they weren't all murders – many of his victims were raped. Those were the assaults that he was convicted of in 1982. However, it's very likely, I believe, that there were other crimes, perhaps even unreported ones, involving him. He was certainly one of the UK's most prolific killers; and it's astonishing to think that at the time he was active in carrying out his attacks, there was another Scottish killer, in the shape of Peter Tobin, travelling around the UK, targeting young women and girls.

As I've said, unlike Sinclair, Tobin chose to bury his victims. He even transported bodies hundreds of miles in the boot of his car in order to conceal them under the ground. That he did this to one body he'd already cut in two demonstrates a particularly horrible disregard for human life; but at the outset of his career as a killer, Tobin showed signs of being an opportunistic killer rather than an organized one.

Take the case of the two fourteen-year-old girls who he was prepared to leave in his own flat and set on fire. Not someone else's, or even an empty public building, which anyone could have got into, but the flat of a man who had previous convictions for offences against children. It shows that he hadn't really considered the end result of his attacks on them; he assaulted the two girls and thought about the consequences later. You could argue that it shows he wasn't particularly bright, but this is the nature of an opportunistic crime. It's all about the fine lines; sometimes the pieces fall into place in just the right way for the offender, and sometimes they don't. In this instance, they very clearly didn't; but in the case of Jessie Earl, they very obviously did.

Strong evidence would suggest that Jessie Earl's murder was committed by Peter Tobin, and that it was an opportunistic crime.

Consider the dates, first. Because Jessie's remains weren't discovered for so long, and because her initial disappearance was treated as if she were missing, rather than the victim of a violent crime, it's easy to lose sight of how she fits into Peter Tobin's criminal chronology.

Tobin was known to have stabbed the woman who became his first wife, and they were married in 1969. In 1984, he was reported to have raped an eight-year-old, over a two-month period, in Portsmouth. In 1994, he is jailed for the attack on the two young girls; in 2005, the year after he is released from jail, he attacks another young woman but he flees before the police can catch him. Under an assumed name, he works in a church in Scotland where, in 2006, he meets and kills Angelika Kluk. Following that arrest, the police discover the remains of his other victims. Vicky Hamilton went missing in 1991; her body was found in the garden of his house in Kent in 2007. Dinah McNicol also went missing in 1991; her remains, too, were found in that garden.

There are moments in every police officer's career that stand out. I feel sure that whoever the officer was who knocked on a man's door to ask if he could recall much about the Scotsman who lived next to him will never forget the moment he was told that yes, the neighbour could remember the time Tobin started digging a big hole in the garden, said it was a sandpit for his son but then, oddly, filled it in. Or the moment when they thought they were digging for Dinah's body, only to unearth Vicky's first.

How did Tobin learn to conceal his victims like that? Had he already gained some experience?

The disappearance of Jessie Earl, in 1980, also bears all the hallmarks of an opportunistic crime. Jessie would have been alone, expecting to take a short walk around Beachy Head in the mid-May evening light before returning to her flat. The area would have been quiet – that was why she was there – and someone walking along the coast, someone with the criminal mind of Peter Tobin, would have seen the ideal victim. Using her own underwear to tie her arms behind her back was something Tobin later did to his other victims. At this stage in his 'career', he hadn't yet developed the technique of burying the body, but he concealed it very well indeed, hiding it in deep undergrowth. So well hidden that it might as well have been buried. Jessie's remains lay there, undisturbed, for nine years.

If only her disappearance had been treated as murder. If only the bra used to restrain her had been kept, so that DNA could have been recovered from it. While soil around her remains was gathered at the time, it too was disposed of because the case wasn't declared a murder investigation. Soil can also retain traces of DNA from sweat, blood or other bodily fluids; fibres could have fallen off clothing; footprints might be visible; litter such as cigarette butts might still have been around the body. DNA is pretty resilient. I can't stress this enough: the failure to classify Jessie Earl's death as a murder in 1989 is a massive police blunder.

Taking place in 1980, the attack on Jessie would have been one of the first murders Tobin committed, as far as we know. Like many repeat offenders – Tony Holland, for example, in Chapter 11 – he would learn from what he'd done, refine his techniques to repeat the thrill he'd received from the first attack, but would minimize the risk he'd brought upon himself.

Louise Kay's disappearance too bears all the hallmarks of Peter Tobin: the same opportunism; him coming across her, alone, in a place where he could observe potential victims, women of the right age and build. He had the ability to get rid of the car. We can put him in the locality at that point in time. And he's a killer.

It's Louise Kay's missing car that proves to me that she was killed, and is not simply missing. How could it have vanished? When I was a fresh-faced police officer, just out of training and on the beat, I'd walk around my patch and, if I saw a car that looked strange, in a strange place, I'd do a PNC (Police National Computer) check on it. I'd call it in, and wait for a response from base. Back they would come – the car was stolen 200 miles away, it's been dumped there. Given the distinctive nature of Louise's vehicle – the white-painted door on a gold car – it would have stuck out like a sore thumb and have been seen. Someone would have had a report put on the PNC had it been found, but there's nothing in any of the records. It's vanished.

It has to mean that that car, in a fairly short space of time – the tax was due in eight months and wasn't renewed, so it wasn't sitting untaxed somewhere, left on the side of the road – has to have been destroyed. Who had the ability to destroy it? We know that Peter Tobin could have done, through his connections in the car trade and in wrecking yards up and down the country.

This is why I believe Peter Tobin is guilty of killing Jessie Earl, and even more convinced that he later killed Louise Kay. What are the chances of both of these crimes being committed in such close proximity, at Beachy Head, by an 'unknown' person, when we know that a serial killer, who chose victims like these two young women, lived and carried out his crimes in the area? I take the unfinished nature of this investigation personally; I want to see it concluded. More than anything, I want justice for the families of the two young women.

Unfortunately, the system of justice doesn't always deliver.

10

MISCARRIAGES OF JUSTICE: MINDY SANGHERA, ANDREW KEMP, JILL DANDO, OSCAR PISTORIUS

PUTTING SOMEONE IN JAIL IS TOUGH. GETTING someone out is even tougher. A case I've recently become involved in runs in the complete opposite direction to my usual investigative route. Typically, I'm presented with evidence, sometimes with a suspect; there's a body, perhaps a murder weapon; there might be a couple of cases of police files to go through; and there might be some forensic reports that will assist in identifying a suspect or group of suspects. The grieving family will be glad of my assistance and we'll work together towards collating enough evidence to allow the police to arrest a suspect and hopefully secure a conviction against them.

Like I say, a typical case. But not so in this instance. This murder happened some time ago. There's a murder weapon, and a clear motive has been established for the suspect to carry out the crime. The suspect has also been identified, arrested, tried and convicted. The family of the deceased victim believes the correct person has been jailed and is not interested in any attempt to reopen the case. The person convicted of the killing is in jail for life, serving a minimum fourteen-year term. It is her family who has contacted me for my help.

I believe there's been a miscarriage of justice in this instance and I'm determined to prove that the woman in jail is innocent of the crime of murder.

The reason I feel this is the case is, in part, to do with the discrepancies between the pathology reports and the crime scene photographs. The reports describe a chaotic murder involving defensive wounds and forty-three knife cuts, some deep, to the victim's body. The photos, on the other hand, show an orderly room with no signs of the chaos indicated in the written reports.

Harmohinder – known as Mindy – Sanghera was studying to be a dental technician at the University of Birmingham. A straight-A student, she was in the third year of her course when, in May 2007, she was arrested for the killing of Sana Ali, wife of Sair Ali. Sair Ali was Mindy's boyfriend; he had married his cousin in 2006, despite having had a relationship with

Mindy for the previous two years. Sana, eight years younger than her husband, was eleven weeks pregnant at the time she was killed. She was only seventeen.

On the day Sana died, 11 May, Mindy had gone to see her to tell her about Sair and the relationship she had with him. She told her parents that she'd been to see Sana when she got home later that day. When she heard that Sana had been found dead, she contacted the police to let them know she had been at the house on the 11th and had spoken to Sana.

Mindy's account is that she went to the house and entered through the back door. She had told three people she was going to see Sana, including her friend Sheetal who she contacted on her mobile just before she went inside. When she stepped into the house, at Sana's invitation, she removed her shoes by the back door. Again, knowing Sana was pregnant, Mindy offered to close the kitchen window which required her to climb up on to the counter in her bare feet.

Mindy says she then told Sana about her relationship with Sair, but that Sana already knew he was having an affair. However, she had thought it was with someone else. Sana reportedly told Mindy that she coped with the stress of her marriage by cutting herself.

A 2018 report on self-harming published in the *BMJ* suggests that incidences of self-harm have been rising steadily over the past two decades. By far the largest category of self-harmers is teenage girls. Tragically, this same study suggested that those who self-harmed were nine times more likely to kill themselves 'in the follow-up period' after self-harming.

Having spoken with Sana, Mindy left and Sana locked the door behind her. Mindy then rang her friend Sheetal again before making her way home.

Mobile phone analysis shows that between 2.15 p.m. and roughly 4.07 p.m., when Sana's sister-in-law came to the house, twenty-one calls and texts were made or sent to Sana by various members of her family. The 999 call made at 4.07 p.m. by the sister-in-law was recorded: 'I think I've just found out my sister-in-law's killing herself, killed herself, I don't know.' A doctor said in their police statement that when the paramedics arrived, Sana was still warm and within the time frame to resuscitate her.

The prosecution's case was that Mindy arrived, persuaded Sana to let her in, stabbed her, and then left by the back kitchen window, which would account for the locked door.

The case against Mindy mainly hinged on her footprint on the counter by the window. However, there are only two prints; one facing toward the window, the other facing back into the room, which is consistent with Mindy's account of putting one foot up there to shut the window, as requested by Sana. There's no forensic evidence of any kind to show that Mindy actually climbed through the window – there were 123 forensic traces found on the blinds and window, and none matched Mindy's DNA. A video was made by Mindy's father, showing someone of Mindy's height and build trying to leave the house via the window. It proved that it was impossible to do so without leaving some sort of forensic trace.

The police suggested that due to the nature of her studies, Mindy had access to the kind of overalls familiar to anyone who watches TV crime dramas such as *CSI* or *Waking the Dead*. Mindy did not have blood on her hands or clothes because, they claimed, she wore a full forensic suit, with a mask, two pairs of gloves, and white booties to cover her shoes. They claim she disposed of this suit in an incinerator at the hospital she visited and would have been familiar with as part of her course at the university. There is no evidence to support any of these assertions.

The trial was conducted on the basis that Sana had been murdered rather than taking her own life; meaning there had to be a killer – either Mindy or another, unknown, party. The case against Mindy Sanghera was largely based on circumstantial evidence; there was no forensic proof directly linking Mindy to Sana. The knife, left at the scene next to Sana's body, could have been bought anywhere in the Birmingham area, cannot be connected to Mindy, and doesn't have her prints or any of her DNA.

However, by a majority verdict, Mindy was found guilty and sentenced to life in prison.

Sair, who admitted in court to having 'sinned', has left the country 'to try and start [his] life again'.

There are a number of factors relating to the way evidence was collected and used in the trial that I find troubling. Most obviously is the crime scene itself – a bedroom in the house – and this is where the evidence I've looked at can be interpreted in different ways. The scene-of-crime photos show an orderly scene, with pools of blood all in one area. There is little disturbance of the bed, contrasting with the chaotic scene described in the autopsy reports of defensive wounds and a violent struggle, and no transfer of blood out of the bedroom.

A blood-pattern expert has looked at the scene-of-crime photos and observed that the blood pools suggest that Sana was sat on the edge of the bed, bleeding from cuts on her arms. She has two severe wounds: one to her chest, one to her abdomen. This expert thinks that Sana fell back on the bed after the chest injury, but sat up again, pulled up her top and bent forward when the abdominal injury was inflicted. She then fell to the floor and blood pooled underneath her (it was mixed with abdominal fluid) before she rolled over on to her back and was found in that position by the paramedics.

Earlier that day, Mindy had filled up her car with

petrol, and the CCTV images from the garage show her wearing the same clothes as those she wore later on when visiting Sana, clothes which were then placed on the back of her chair at home and recovered when she was arrested three days after Sana's death. No item of Mindy's clothing was shown to be carrying any of Sana's blood. The police have no evidence that she wore the protective clothing they suggest she did.

This is just one element of the case that I don't feel was addressed satisfactorily. Why, for instance, were so many calls and attempts made to contact Sana that afternoon? Was it because the family were genuinely worried she might seriously harm herself?

Analysis of Sana's mobile phone suggests that it was used to make calls, not just receive them, after Mindy had left the house (we know when she left because of the time of her call to her friend Sheetal). Who made these calls?

Mindy herself told her parents she'd been to visit Sana; she also told the police. With so little forensic evidence at the scene, and none linking her to the actual death, why would she willingly incriminate herself in this way? And why, if she had brought and used a special forensic suit, would she take it off to leave her footprints by the kitchen window? A window that showed no forensic evidence of her having climbed through it, and with no damaged blinds. The police needed to prove that Mindy had used the window as her exit, because – with the front door being locked from the inside – that was the only way they could safely claim that Sana was dead before Mindy left.

David Wells and I will present submissions to the Criminal Cases Review Commission (CCRC) shortly, with a view to having Mindy's conviction reviewed. Our ultimate aim is to have her case referred back to the Court of Appeal, and for her conviction to be overturned. The CCRC is an independent body set up to review miscarriages of justice. The test applied by the CCRC when reviewing a case is to establish whether or not there is a 'real possibility' that if a case were referred to the Court of Appeal, the court would regard the conviction as unsafe. I have always felt strongly that Mindy is innocent, and that her conviction is unsafe. There are too many unanswered questions, with an outcome that makes no sense. The submissions we'll make to the CCRC ought to meet their test and, ultimately, I hope we'll get Mindy's conviction overturned.

Another case I'm involved in and am including here is the polar opposite. Andrew Kemp deserves to be in jail, but for a different crime than the one he was convicted of.

The story of Andrew Kemp, sentenced to a minimum term of twenty-two years in jail for the murder of Leighann Wightman in 2011, is an extraordinary tale of official incompetence. That she died angers me because her death was totally avoidable. Not only because she'd taken out a restraining order against Kemp, but also because he should never have been freely walking the streets of Nottingham in the first place.

Kemp is originally from Scotland. In 1999, when he was living in Nottingham, he was jailed for rape. Upon his release, he formed a relationship with Leighann Wightman, who was about half his age. In 2010, she took out a restraining order against him after he pleaded guilty to common assault on her; Kemp was sentenced to a two-year community order and instructed to attend a two-year domestic abuse programme.

Kemp clearly couldn't control his anger around women. He also seemed to have some effect on Leighann, because she didn't stop seeing him during the two-year order and he would regularly spend the night at her home in Netherfield, in the east of Nottingham, which she shared with her young daughter.

On the day she died, Kemp was in a bar with a friend, Lee Brown. Brown showed Kemp a text he'd received from Leighann which read, 'Are you free? We could do something.' She also sent one to Kemp saying, 'LOL, my door open for you . . . coz I love you.'

Kemp carried on drinking, went on to a nightclub with Brown where he danced with two women, and returned to Leighann's home just before 1.30 a.m. on Saturday, 15 October.

Kemp claims that when he told Leighann about the two women in the club, she grabbed a knife and attacked him. He says he took it off her and stabbed her himself, inflicting twenty-seven knife wounds. He told the police that he'd been frightened by her actions, had lost control and would plead guilty to manslaughter.

CCTV, however, shows that Kemp arrived at Leighann's house and left again fourteen minutes later, giving a clear timeline. Leighann was heard by neighbours to scream, 'Get off me,' at least twice. The jury believed the prosecution's case, that Kemp had been incensed by the text Lee Brown had received, and had reacted towards Leighann the way he was known to have done with women in the past when angry and fuelled by alcohol: with extreme violence.

It's devastating for Leighann's family that she met her end in this way, and it's hard to imagine how her daughter's life can be put back together after being ripped apart in this way. However, and this is where I came to be involved, he shouldn't have been in Nottingham in the first place, free to commit rape, free to assault Leighann, and free to kill her. Because he'd killed before, and had got away with it.

In Falkirk, Scotland, in 1993, Kemp had killed Norah Smith, a sixty-four-year-old grandmother. He was tried for the crime but the charge was found 'not proven' by the jury; as a result, he was free to leave Scotland and relocate south of the border in Nottingham.

Norah Smith was a neighbour of Kemp. As it was New Year's Eve, Kemp was hosting a party at his flat. Kemp believed, wrongly, that Norah was taking some strong prescription drugs, diazepam, or 'jellies' – often seen by drug abusers as a cheaper substitute for heroin – and Kemp decided he wanted them for himself. She couldn't help him. Witnesses present at the party that night saw him come and go from his flat a few times; at one point he emerged from the bathroom, wearing only a towel, and shoved his clothes into the washing machine, which he proceeded to put on a boil wash.

When he wasn't in his flat he had gone into Norah Smith's home to steal from her. He had attacked her, hit her around the head and tried to strangle her, before tying a ligature around her neck and killing her. He then set fire to the papers and furniture in her flat to try to cover up the evidence of his involvement in the crime. Although he denied ever having been on the premises, his palm print was found on the inside of her toilet door.

After the trial, Kemp boasted of the crime and told three different people details that only the killer could have known about the murder, yet somehow he had managed to persuade a jury to find the charge 'not proven'.

Following Kemp's trial for Leighann Wightman's murder, Norah Smith's family tried to get the police and the CPS to revisit Norah's case to see if Kemp could be successfully prosecuted for her murder.

Naturally, they faced a few obstacles, chief of which was the issue of double jeopardy. As with the case of serial killer Angus Sinclair, strict requirements have to be met before a new trial against the same offender is opened. Among those criteria is the emergence of compelling new evidence. In Angus Sinclair's case, this was certainly available. Unfortunately, in Norah Smith's case, there could be no retrial of Andrew Kemp for her murder because all the original court papers from his trial had gone missing or – I believe – been destroyed. The judge who conducted the original trial had passed away, and his contemporaneous private notes, made in court during the trial, were sketchy and in places indecipherable. The CPS had the opportunity to speak to him before his death, but didn't do so.

Norah Smith's family were understandably devastated that the promise of a retrial was found to be impossible, and this is when they turned to me for assistance. Unfortunately for them, there's no sign of there being copies of the trial papers anywhere in the system. There's little that I can do to force the issue to be addressed and for a new trial to be opened without those original papers – it's difficult to argue the validity of 'new' evidence when you haven't got the 'old' evidence with which to compare it.

I've looked at this case a number of times now – I've even been to visit Kemp's old flat in Falkirk. Sadly, although it's clear to me that Andrew Kemp is guilty of Norah Smith's death, it's also clear that he will never be convicted of it – unless we can get the law changed to allow him to be tried again for a crime he's already been acquitted of. And that's something I'm fighting for. It may take a long time, it may never happen, but I want to carry on trying, for Norah and her family – just in the same way I continue to fight for a new inquest and some justice for Jessie Earl's family.

Someone else who I believe will never be convicted of their crime is Jill Dando's killer. Much has been written about Jill Dando's death, and some of it is quite extraordinarily fanciful. I made a TV programme, *The Dando Files*, in June 2015 for the *Mirror* about the murder, and my conclusions about the crime are the same as many of the commentators who have written about her death since the man convicted of it, Barry George, was released from prison after a court found that he had been wrongly convicted in the first place.

Jill Dando was a hugely popular BBC presenter. She'd fronted the *Breakfast News*, *Holiday*, *Crimewatch* and the *Six O'Clock News*, among many other shows. She'd come to the BBC in London from their offices in the south-west, and lived in Fulham. On the morning of 26 April 1999, she returned home after spending the night at her fiancé's house in nearby Chiswick. She reached her house shortly after 11.30 a.m., and police believe she was shot and killed immediately upon arrival at her own front door.

Her body wasn't discovered for another fourteen minutes; one neighbour had heard a short, sudden shout, but no gunfire. Two local people noticed a man striding down the road shortly after the time Dando was believed to have been shot – a tall, well-dressed man wearing a Barbour-style jacket and carrying a mobile phone.

The reason no one heard gunfire is because the killer, after forcing Dando down on the step so that her face was almost touching the stone, placed the gun close to her left temple. According to the forensic expert, this meant that the gases that normally cause the sound of the explosion would be mostly absorbed by the side of her head. It also meant there wouldn't be much blood and matter splashing back to cover the attacker. The attack was fast and professional; Jill Dando was a target, this was something the perpetrator had done before, and he knew how to draw the minimum amount of attention to himself while going about his business.

It's hard to see how the police went from possessing this knowledge to deciding to pick on Barry George as the likely culprit. Admittedly, it was a year before George was arrested and the investigation became focused on him, but it's hard to understand what they saw in him when they were looking for someone who fitted the description of a determined, effective and cold-blooded hitman.

Barry George had problems. He had already come to the attention of the police when he made it on to one of their lists as being a potential danger to members of the Royal Family, and he apparently had an obsession with Princess Diana. He was reported to hang around the streets of west London trying to direct traffic; he had supposedly charged into a relative's house, for a prank, and fired a blank starting pistol, as if conducting a raid. According to one account, he had pretended to be a cousin of Freddie Mercury when the singer died; and he lived in a flat that, so said another source, 'resembled a junk yard', with newspapers and clothing strewn everywhere.

None of these were the worst of Barry George's problems. Nor was his epilepsy. Unfortunately, someone had decided that he fitted a certain psychological profile, and that he must be the man guilty of Jill Dando's murder. Never mind there was almost no evidence linking him to Dando, let alone her death; it wasn't even possible to say that Barry George knew where Jill Dando lived. His coat bore a tiny particle that *could* have been from explosive material, but no effort was made to ascertain where the coat might have come into contact with explosives. And, in the absence of a murder weapon, no explanation that made sense was given as to how Barry George had managed to rid himself of the gun.

After considering all of this, you'd be amazed that Barry George was found guilty at his trial in 2001, but, thanks to a majority verdict, that's exactly what happened. I'd say the only thing Barry George was guilty of was being mentally ill. He had a history of medical problems and had told the police he suffered from a personality disorder, but that didn't seem to count in his case.

Nevertheless, after a retrial in 2008, Barry George was acquitted and, at this point, new theories about Jill Dando's death started to circulate more widely.

At the initial trial, Michael Mansfield, QC, acting in Barry George's defence, had made his own allegations about the possible killer or killers. He suggested that Dando's death was a revenge killing, carried out by a Serb gunman acting in retaliation for an attack on a Serb TV station which had killed sixteen people. While it wouldn't have been the first time foreign agents have acted on the streets of Britain (following the Russian killing of the dissident writer Georgi Markov in Balham, London, in 1978), nor the last (given the Salisbury poisonings of the Skripals in 2018), Mansfield's suggestion appeared at the time a little far-fetched. It was also pointed out that the TV station was bombed only four days before Jill Dando was killed.

I do think there is something in what he said, however. There is no doubt it was a professional killing, but there are one or two other clues that should be considered. The bullet that was recovered showed very little rifling on its side. Rifling on the inside of a barrel – marks which transfer to a bullet when it's fired – is needed to help the bullet spin, creating greater accuracy through its trajectory. In a short-range weapon, when used close to a target, no such rifling would be required. In the UK, following the mass shootings in Hungerford and Dunblane, new gun laws were brought in which resulted in the deactivation of many old guns; deactivated weapons usually have no rifling inside the barrel.

This was suggested by the police at the time of Barry George's first trial – that he had taken a deactivated weapon and repurposed it for his use. It could also be true of any criminal in the UK, however – taking a deactivated gun and restoring it. It's not as outlandish as it might sound, to consider the prospect of a weapon that had been deactivated being used in a crime such as this; in 2004, a father-and-son team were convicted of selling over 3,000 weapons together with instructions on how to overcome the problem of deactivation. Three years after the pair were convicted, their guns had been recovered from sixty-five crime scenes, including eight murders.

It's therefore possible that the gun *was* something accessible to a criminal here in the UK, despite our strict gun laws. But does anyone seriously think that Barry George would be able to get hold of a reactivated gun, kill Jill Dando with it, get away without being seen and somehow dispose of the weapon afterwards (it's never been recovered, remember), and, crucially, without telling anyone what he'd done? I would say without any hesitation: no.

The Dando murder is a classic case of one narrative thread being followed to the exclusion of all others. Someone decided Barry George could be guilty, and so looked at the evidence that supported this theory, discarding the rest of it. They decided the murder displayed signs of being committed by a loner, a man with serious psychological problems, someone known to the authorities for having a history of problems with women. Barry George fitted the bill, but what swam into the consciousness of the team working the murder first: the theory of the 'lone nutter', or the appearance of Barry George on the police's radar?

In the police file to which I managed to gain exclusive access for my investigation, I found a significant lead that was never followed up: one or more men carried out the attack on the orders of one of the UK's most notorious criminal gangs, and the weapon used was then dismantled and chucked into a canal, never to be found. More recently, I've received information that suggests there is more likely to be a connection between the gunman and Serbia than between the gunman and organized crime, but that there is overlap between the two.

With no DNA trace left anywhere near the crime scene, and no one able to identify the man seen walking along the road after Jill Dando was killed, her murder looks like a professional hit in every respect. I'm sure the killer would have no qualms about killing again if they thought they were going to be caught, which would cause anyone to think twice about approaching them. What is abundantly clear is that Barry George can have played no part in a crime such as this and was rightly acquitted of the charges laid against him.

One of the most extraordinary – and even more high-profile – cases I've been involved in is where there is no doubt about the guilt of the man in jail. Why I've included it here, in a chapter about miscarriages of justice, is because I think he's in jail for the wrong reasons, and probably serving the sentence he is because of who he is, rather than what he did. I'm talking about the case of one of the best-known figures in sport, the downfall of Oscar Pistorius.

A key thing I realized when dealing with Oscar Pistorius was how the justice system – at least in South Africa, but I suspect all over the world – reacts to having a celebrity in the dock. Justice is supposed to be blind, but while we would all like to believe that, I'm not sure it's true; money certainly talks, but does fame alter the picture too? Would someone else, someone without Oscar Pistorius's international status and reputation, be treated by the courts the way he was? Convicted of one offence, sentenced, then convicted at appeal of another offence, and his sentence doubled at appeal? I'm not sure. It sounds to me like the court of public opinion having its say after the actual, legal court, and I think that's a dangerous precedent to set.

Oscar Pistorius's case is a remarkable one. In 2013, three of the most famous people in the world were South African. Obviously, Nelson Mandela, President of South Africa from 1994 to 1999, after spending twenty-eight years in jail, is the best known. And Archbishop Desmond Tutu, recipient of the Nobel Peace Prize in 1984, is also a familiar figure on the world stage. Then there's Oscar Pistorius; born with missing bones in his feet, which were then amputated when he was still a baby, Oscar became one of the world's more recognized athletes and the 'face' of the Parasport movement as a result of the prosthetics he wore, the 'blades'.

The short version of Oscar Pistorius's dramatic fall from grace in the early hours of 14 February 2013 is this: Oscar was in his bedroom with his girlfriend, Reeva Steenkamp (they'd been together for a relatively short amount of time, about six months). What happened early that morning is not in doubt: Reeva Steenkamp got out of bed and went into the bathroom. Oscar, hearing a noise that he said alarmed him, reached for the handgun he kept beside the bed and fired it through the bathroom door, believing that Reeva was still in bed next to him and intruders were breaking into the house. Reeva died instantly.

Oscar Pistorius killed Reeva Steenkamp. The question is: did he mean to?

When the story broke, it was massive news around the world. Being particularly keen on sport, I was interested in Oscar and his achievements anyway, but I think we probably all knew something about him before that point.

While the investigation into Reeva's death was still at an early stage – a few weeks after Reeva's killing – Lesley Gardiner, my producer, proposed we make contact with Oscar's team to see if they would cooperate in making a programme with us. Although I knew almost every broadcaster in the world was trying to do the exact same thing, I thought it was a good idea.

I spoke to his PR person and outlined the sorts of things we could do if they offered us access to Oscar. I suggested that the team and I, in addition to an interview with Oscar, would carry out an investigation, just as we would carry out an investigation into a killing in the UK. We'd look at some of the aspects of the police case which were being talked about – they'd said Pistorius had put on his blades *before* he shot Reeva, that sort of thing.

She explained that we were in a queue of competing media interests and outlined some of those ahead of us: ABC, *Oprah*, *60 Minutes*; all the big players. It was quite clear that I was in a fire pit with the biggest media outlets there were, and little lowly me had just made a pitch for ITV, saying we could make an especially good programme with him. I thought, 'Well, no point in giving up now,' so I carried on the dialogue and, to my surprise, it soon emerged that she actually quite liked what I was suggesting.

Right up to the start date of the first trial, March 2014, the PR agent and I were talking on and off. As I was driving back home one Friday, after visiting a crime scene in the north of England, I got a phone call from her.

'Look,' she said. 'I can't tell you it will be a deal, but what I can say to you is, if you wanted to come over next week, I think it would be very worthwhile for you.'

I spoke to ITV, who thought it was worth the risk. I jumped on a plane two days later and, after flying into Johannesburg, drove straight to Oscar's lawyer's office. There I met with the lawyers, the PR agent and Oscar's uncle, Arnold.

I thought we had a done deal, as I'd flown over with

the expectation that the family wanted to look me in the eye, see what I was like, and would then agree to my proposal. Everything about the conversations the PR agent and I had had up till then led me to believe this. So I was incredibly surprised to find that I was wrong.

The family, it turned out, didn't need convincing; they wanted the programme to happen, they liked what we'd suggested, but it was the lawyers who weren't so convinced.

'Mark, look, we just can't do it before trial,' they said to me.

The family had to go with the lawyers' view – that doing something with us might prejudice what they wanted to say at the trial. They wanted to put forward all their evidence in a court.

I thought they were wrong then, and I still think they're wrong today. They didn't challenge any of the untruths that came out. The police put lots of stories into the public domain which were inaccurate – worse, were downright lies. The Pistorius camp never countered them or corrected them at the time, so in the absence of any kind of challenge, of any kind of narrative coming out of the Pistorius camp that told a different story, these falsehoods became truths, despite being untrue.

Even after I had flown back to the UK, I continued to talk to the Pistorius family. I was certain that no matter the outcome for Oscar there would be a programme that we could make at some point. This determination paid off, because out of the blue in early 2016 I received a text message from Arnold when I was at home one day: 'Are you still up for doing an interview? Let's do it.'

I hastily contacted ITV and said, 'We're on.'

I spent a weekend in South Africa, talking to the family, and to Oscar, for a long time. Arnold showed me the letters from all the big US media outlets, all offering big sums to do this, film that – while we weren't offering anything. We simply said we'd carry out an interview.

'You never gave up,' Arnold said to me, 'and your persistence is one of the reasons we're working with you. It's not the main reason, but it's one of the reasons why we came back to you. That and the way you said you are going to do your programme, as a very fair programme. Sitting there and putting the evidence out, not taking a side either way.'

Once we had the commission from ITV I went back with the crew to South Africa to start filming. Like many of my projects, we had to keep it under wraps. We couldn't let the UK media know we were going or where we were filming, and we had to be discreet in South Africa as well.

That's not as straightforward as it might sound. Clearly we couldn't film at locations relevant to the case, pointing cameras at everything while I stood in

front of them and talked the investigation through –
that would have been an open invitation to the police
to come and ask what the hell we thought we were
doing. So we decided to do the essential filming of the
interview with Oscar first, in case we were invited to
leave the country at any point.

By then, the original police investigator on the case
had been replaced, so some of the stories they'd put
out initially had been retracted. However, there still
remained many things to refute, and I thought we
could start that process by asking Oscar some direct
questions. We could then do follow-up footage as
needed later on. At that time, Oscar was out of jail on
bail in a two-bedroomed flat in the garden of his uncle
Arnold; Arnold's house was particularly large. I prepared for the interview by talking to Oscar in his flat,
while the team remained in the main house, setting
up to do actual filming with Oscar.

All of a sudden, Oscar's aunt came down. 'Correctional Services are here,' she told him.

As Oscar was out on bail, he was wearing a tag,
which was faulty and kept setting off an alarm. He
had complained and a Correctional Services team had
been sent out to fix it. As it was Oscar Pistorius, the
team, so his aunt said, included the head of Correctional Services, who'd arrived with a four-person-strong
entourage.

I remember thinking, 'If you were in the UK and

your tag went off, you'd have to wait ages for someone to show up, and even then he'd probably be an
apprentice.' This was one of the main indications that
the way this case was being treated was not like any
other.

'Hang on – I shouldn't be here when they come in,'
I said to Oscar and his aunt.

I was concerned not so much for us as for Oscar;
although he was allowed to do an interview, I thought
someone might object to the sight of a UK camera
crew and, with that as an excuse, would probably put
him back in jail. Legally we might be fine, but in practice anything might happen.

'Where should I go?' I ran on the spot, looking
around at the rooms near by. 'Do I go into the bedroom? Do I hide? Will they come in here?' A moment's
thought and I said, 'I'll go up to the top.'

I dashed out of the flat and towards the main house,
right up to the top where the crew were setting up. 'No
one's going to come all the way up there,' I thought. I
opened the door to the landing area we were going to
use, to find the whole crew lying down on the floor.
We'd taken quite a big team with us, so the floor was
just a mass of bodies. Everyone looked up at me.

'Why is everyone on the floor?' I asked.

They waved hurriedly at me to keep quiet, and to lie
down too. Someone pointed and whispered, 'They're
just outside there.'

Immediately beyond the other entrance to the room, on a staircase, was where Correctional Services had positioned themselves.

I joined them on the floor and remained as quiet as possible. Then I whispered, 'Yes, but they can see our lights from here.'

We'd brought some portable studio lights with us, so as to get a good picture, and they were visible through the windows. Acting together, the crew and I carefully slid some big blackout boards we'd also brought with us across the room and up against the windows, one at a time, so that Correctional Services – or anyone else who might be trying to peer in – couldn't see us. We had to wait there, on the floor, without moving much, for two hours, until Correctional Services finally left.

Afterwards, I checked with Oscar's lawyer, who assured me that he wouldn't have been sent back to jail if he'd been seen in our company, but we couldn't have known that at the time. There was a lot of anger towards Oscar in South Africa, and I think the system could well have decided that they would put him back in jail to prevent any public outcry about special treatment.

If anything, I think the treatment of Oscar worked the other way; so keen not to be seen to be handling him with kid gloves, the authorities treated him harshly. In the end, that's what happened; after the first trial, when he was found guilty of culpable homicide, he was sent to prison for five years. There was an outcry, and at the appeal in November 2015 Oscar Pistorius was found guilty of murder. After more courtroom appearances and lengthy arguments, finally, in November 2017, he was sentenced to fifteen years in jail, less time served.

I can find no evidence that says he deliberately shot through the bathroom door in his bedroom, believing the noise he'd heard to be Reeva. The two of them had been seeing each other for six months; they were still in the courting phase of their relationship and by all accounts were very close.

What he did was wrong, you can't get away from that – he killed somebody. But when I spoke to Oscar about that, he said to me, 'I have to live with that for the rest of my life. I've killed someone that I love. I have to live with that.'

He knew for certain that he was shooting at someone, probably even killing them. He didn't think it was his girlfriend, though – he thought it was an intruder. That was his point, and after studying the submissions seen at the trial I think there's strong evidence to support that. Judge Masipa, the original judge, believed that too, which was where the sentence of culpable homicide came from. There was no evidence to show that he deliberately set out to kill Reeva. There are questions, of course, that need answers: when Oscar was woken up by the noise in the bathroom, why didn't he check whether Reeva was beside him? Why didn't he turn the light on? Why did he shoot into a door which was shut?

It was interesting talking to people about it when we returned to the UK. I explained that, to assess whether or not Oscar's reaction to hearing what he thought was the noise of an intruder was an appropriate one, they had to understand Johannesburg and the situation there for many householders. Coming from a culture where we have very little legitimate contact with firearms, I felt it necessary to explain the whole concept of firearms over there, and house invasions. How there are people who break into people's homes, steal guns and use them to shoot the occupants. As a result, it often happens that the occupants will shoot any offenders who come into the house.

There's an incredibly sad case over there of a former South African rugby player, Rudi Visagie, who was woken up by his wife just before dawn one morning in May 2004. His daughter's car was being driven off the driveway – the family had, in recent months, had two cars stolen from their property. Visagie, thinking the car was being stolen by a thief, grabbed his gun and fired through the open bedroom window. However, the driver of the vehicle was his nineteen-year-old daughter, on her way to surprise her boyfriend on his birthday. She died almost immediately. Visagie wasn't charged with murder, because the prosecutors thought that he had suffered enough torment, and would do so for ever.

'You can't take that bullet back,' he said.

What that does for me is set the scene for Oscar's case. This is how people live in South Africa. Sometimes it has to be shoot before you think, because you're having to respond to a life-or-death situation. In 2016–17, an average of twenty-five cars a day were carjacked in the Johannesburg area; the murder rate in South Africa is ten times higher than in the UK.

If Oscar Pistorius had not had a gun to hand that night, if guns were not so readily available, I believe Reeva would still be alive. We know that because, a few weeks before, someone *had* come into the house and Oscar had gone downstairs, armed, ready to shoot him. It was actually a friend coming to use Oscar's washing machine.

At the time, Oscar said that he'd pulled out his gun and went, in his words, 'code red and combat mode', when he heard the noise downstairs. In a stressful moment, with his heart pounding from adrenaline, that was his default reaction. Bear in mind too that he is an elite athlete, who is practised in making split-second decisions, which I think should not be underestimated. Crucially – and this is particularly significant – he is also someone who lives with extreme vulnerability. He's a man who's a double amputee, and isn't stable on his legs as a result. In fact, he's incredibly unstable in that respect, and it adds to his vulnerability. He'd also had threats made against him, which, I suppose, is to be expected when you're famous. When you bear all these factors in mind, the sum total is a level of vulnerability that few of us can truly understand.

I would say to doubters (and there are many; people seem to gravitate towards the comfort of an ordered conspiracy rather than to the chaotic reality of life) that if you were to put three different people in a room and present them with the same scenario, but leave the firearm out of it, you could almost guarantee that each of those three people would deal with it in a different way. One might run away, another might fight, one might freeze. Take the gun away, and Reeva would still be alive.

11

FENLAND DEATH

Danny Hathaway was a mechanic, servicing vehicles in Northamptonshire where he lived. On Wednesday, 7 February 2007, Danny arranged to meet someone to talk about a land deal, and he went to the meeting with some cash in his pocket as a down payment if the deal proved attractive enough. Danny, a New Age traveller who lived on a site in Gretton Brook Road in Corby with his partner, Diana, and their two children, Sam and Ellie, wasn't going to hang around; he and his family were going skiing the next day, he had things to do, and so he went to the meeting expecting it to be a quick one.

He has not been seen again since.

All of my cases have similarities between them, but there are usually differences – sometimes only subtle ones. This one couldn't have been more different. Normally, I'm presented with a problem; a puzzle that can be unravelled using forensic techniques and good old-fashioned detective work. I'll work with the police and the family, read the file and examine the evidence.

Not this time.

Tony Holland, Danny's killer, a double killer, is already in jail, serving a minimum sentence of thirty-five years. There's no doubt he's guilty, so my investigation isn't into him. The reason for my involvement is that the offender employed a certain amount of cunning in concealing his crime.

I've talked before about how everyone's an expert these days. The popularity of TV shows and podcasts on the subject of crime detection means so many more people are familiar with policing techniques. Shows about old crimes – cold cases – whether fictitious or real, are wildly popular and it's widely assumed that the police can pretty much solve every crime nowadays by painstakingly and forensically investigating all the evidence, often without leaving the laboratory.

Advances in the field of forensics are thought to be the clearest, most obvious sign that no crime can remain unsolved – perhaps people are heavily influenced by the sight of scientists staring into microscopes or fiddling with test tubes. There's one obvious drawback here. The mass of figures on our screens dressed in white paper suits – gloved, masked and booted to avoid contaminating a crime scene – ensures thousands of potential criminals out there are learning how not to leave behind any trace of their involvement in a crime. In the past, I wondered how many criminals learned their methods from watching *CSI*, but recently someone said to me, in reference to my TV shows, that I'm teaching people how to commit the perfect murder. So maybe's it's my fault that offenders are getting canny.

However, there's another way in which an offender learns how to avoid leaving a trace: by having done it before, and learning from what they did wrong. Learn from your mistakes, teachers tell pupils at school; and so it is with some criminals. If you're caught by the police, and see exactly what it is they find when they investigate your involvement with the crime, then – provided you are lucky enough, or cunning enough, to avoid being convicted – you can use that knowledge to avoid any kind of detection when you carry out your next attack.

Tony Holland thought he'd learned from his mistakes. While he was on bail for the murder of Danny Hathaway, he killed another man, Bill O'Connor. He knew how he had been caught first time around: one of four vans belonging to him that were seized by the police was the crime scene. The bloodstain on the van's floor, with the victim's fingerprint stamped in his own blood, told its own story.

He'd tried to be clever, too. Holland killed Danny Hathaway and then drove over to meet the victim's wife, saying he was due to rendezvous with her partner.

He even got her to call Danny's mobile phone 'to see where he was' while he, Holland, stood there, knowing that he'd killed Hathaway for the approximately £3,000 in cash Hathaway had on him when they met. Holland had wanted the money to buy a new caravan.

Danny Hathaway's whereabouts were unknown. As the family were about to set off on their skiing holiday to Austria, the idea that Hathaway was 'missing' was clearly wrong. However, without a body, the CPS weren't convinced they could press forward with the case, so Holland was released on police bail. Nobody knows how Danny Hathaway died, because Holland hasn't spoken to the police about the murder. He hasn't spoken about anything, in fact; it was only when he stood up in court to plead 'not guilty' that detectives heard him speak for the first time.

In an effort to prove that Danny had not simply gone missing from his home, Northamptonshire Police contacted over 1,300 organizations, from the NHS to mobile phone companies and utility firms. None of them had any record of Danny after 7 February. Danny Hathaway had been murdered, and his body, police believed, had been dumped into water somewhere in the myriad canals and ditches that criss-cross the fenland between Peterborough and King's Lynn. Police searches had taken place in a couple of spots – one just off the A43 at Bulwick, less than ten miles from Danny's home, and the other a stretch of water at Saddlebow in Norfolk – but to no avail.

The investigation had obviously made an impression on Holland. He probably hadn't expected to be caught so quickly, but as the last person believed to have seen Danny alive he was obviously the prime suspect. The evidence found in his van – the bloodstain, along with a hammer, spade, metal bar, pickaxe handle, rope, boxing gloves and a knife – was something he understood, and when he decided to kill again he determined not to leave evidence lying about and to do a better job of clearing up.

It's hard to know why someone will kill so freely. From understanding what the murderers I've spoken to have to say, the truth is that once you've murdered someone and not been prosecuted, it's like you've been bitten by the bug. Some people get a certain amount of sexual gratification from it – but I doubt Holland was sexually driven in his killings. It was about money, power and control for him, showing his victims that he was the boss. Some of these people think, 'I can do what I want – hit that person, stab that person – and get away with it.' Then, one day they stab someone who dies – and they still get away with it. How many people might Holland have attacked or stabbed before he killed Danny Hathaway?

Two months after he walked free, Holland lured Bill O'Connor to his van, which was parked in a road behind some shops in Bury St Edmunds. At his trial, Holland implied O'Connor was there for a drug deal; Holland told the court he was driving someone called 'Joe', who met with O'Connor.

'I got out of the van to see if I could recognize anybody and I walked across and I think that Bill recognized me, at which point he started walking towards me and I shook his hand and he said, "What have you got?" And I told him that it was not me he wanted.'

If, as he claimed, Holland was innocent of both the murder and the drug-dealing, it doesn't explain why he tried to obscure the number plate on his van with black tape.

Holland, the prosecution stated, hadn't walked away from the vehicle as he said he had; instead, he'd attempted to get O'Connor inside his van. O'Connor got into the back but quickly saw what was about to happen and jumped out. Holland followed him out on to the street and attacked him, stabbing him eight times – in the eye, the head, the neck and the heart.

When the police investigated this horrific crime, Bill O'Connor's mother remembered Holland approaching her to ask for O'Connor's mobile phone number a week before the attack. He'd even offered to pay her for the information. She told the police and they followed up, using mobile phone records, CCTV and ANPR to track Holland's movements.

When they examined the van Holland had been driving that day, it had been cleared out and there was no sign of any interaction with O'Connor. Until, that is, forensics officers became involved, and identified fibres linking Holland to the killing.

What was Holland's motive this time? He believed O'Connor had 'looked at' his fiancée, Lisa Smith, in the wrong way. When he was on remand, Holland telephoned Smith and, at his trial, the jury was read transcripts of these calls. Holland had said to her, 'I do not care if I get done, knowing what that bastard done to you. Those nightmares he gave you.' And, in another call, 'Please tell me that I am not in here for nothing?'

If O'Connor hadn't jumped out of the van, it's highly likely that Holland would have done to him what he did to Hathaway – killed him and dumped him in water somewhere – and the investigation would have been hampered once again by the absence of a body. Holland would probably still have been convicted of the crime, given the evidence linking him to the last known sighting of O'Connor, and the probability that his efforts to 'clean' his van would still have left forensic evidence; but O'Connor's family would find themselves in the same position as Danny Hathaway's: unable to bury their son and partner.

So, what's my involvement here? A clearly identifiable offender is serving a long jail sentence for his crimes. There are no questions about the evidence that convicted him, and no chance of a successful appeal against that conviction. He almost certainly would have gone on to kill again after those two murders, given that he showed such disdain for life over the sum of £3,000 and a perceived slight on his fiancée. It's a good thing that he will be behind bars for an incredibly long time – there's no doubt that Holland is a nasty piece of work. It's also highly likely that he offended before he attacked Hathaway, although I don't believe he killed anyone before then. He almost certainly had previous for violence, but nothing on the scale of the two murders he committed. Therefore, there are no previous crimes I need to investigate either.

My involvement stems from the fact that I want to help put the final piece of the jigsaw in place, and give Danny Hathaway's family the opportunity they've been seeking for so long: to bury Danny's body properly. Danny's father, Revd Kenneth Hathaway, made a plea for anyone who knows where his son's body is to come forward, so that Danny can have the 'dignity of burial and the respect of a funeral'. Revd Hathaway and the police have repeatedly made appeals, all of which have been unsuccessful.

However, I've been approached by a source who has told me in detail where they believe Danny's body to be. The source has described accurately, as far as I can tell, how Danny Hathaway was killed and how his body was disposed of. Given how dangerous Tony

Holland is, despite being behind bars, I have to protect my source, who will remain anonymous.

What I've been told is this. Holland dumped Danny's body into water off a bridge at the back of a travellers' site. He'd wrapped it up in tarpaulin and tied it to a gearbox (the police had previously been told by a different source it was an engine block, so this new evidence chimes closely with what they know as well).

Acting on this information, I spent some time with a search team from Peter Faulding's SGI organization and we surveyed the areas where I hoped we'd be able to locate Danny's remains. When we were ready, I informed the police that we had new information relating to Danny Hathaway and that we would work with them to make plans to formally undertake the search. We need to make sure we've got the right bridge, the right location.

The police had first searched for Danny's body in a large area of estuary, but they didn't find any sign of it there. I didn't want them to think we were scouting places without their knowledge, so I shared the new information with them at the earliest opportunity, although I told them very little. The agreement I'd made with my source was that I wouldn't even disclose how the murder took place until we were ready to proceed with a full search. That information won't help the police find the body, but it will confirm for them that the source's information is credible. The source is prepared to tell the police everything once they're involved – provided they will afford the source protection.

SGI are, like me, providing their services to the police for free, so there will be no cost to the force in searching for and retrieving the body. We're all happy to be working behind the scenes, trying to help the police get to the point where they can close the file on the case, and give the family back their loved one.

I'm now preparing to take the police to the sites we've identified. We're conducting those visits with their scenes-of-crime officers, their detectives and their press team, and we're setting a provisional date of late May 2019 for the full forensics search to take place – if the weather is kind. Our hope and expectation is that we will at last find Danny's body and help his family through the final stage of this traumatic period.

12

THE HUNT CONTINUES

I'M NO STRANGER TO DEATH. TO ME, IT HAS A UNIQUE smell – I've been to many post-mortems. I've also been in the presence of people who have killed and I've been in rooms where people have been killed. I've seen appalling, awful footage of individuals doing unspeakable things to other human beings. None of that puts me off my aim, though. I want to see those people responsible caught, tried, convicted and sent to jail.

In the past, I've observed that everyone is capable of killing, which often surprises those to whom I've said this – but it's true. I know this because I've dealt with so many people whom I'd never have thought capable of killing someone – yet they have. It depends on the circumstances and the level of provocation someone faces, but there have been a number of times when I've seen a look of shock and horror on someone's face because they've done something they never thought they could.

People fascinate me. I love to sit in a coffee shop and look out of the window, watching people walking past – it's something I've done since joining the police force. On trains, I observe people and I wonder what they're about, what jobs they do, what motivates them, where they are coming from or going to. There are people out there who have completely different lives from us – criminals – about which we know nothing. They are complex, and I'm always studying them, trying to figure out why they do what it is they're doing, however minor it appears – talking to a friend, staring at their phone, tapping away at a laptop . . .

But what those people who commit crimes say to themselves, to allow them to do what they do, remains a mystery. As a police officer, I stopped someone in a car once – we were already observing him – to find the vehicle's interior covered with blood. Not a few drops, but covered. He was, he told us, driving the car because he'd been asked to. Did he not think the blood was a reason not to? we asked him. No, he hadn't really thought about it, he was taking the car to be scrapped, that's all he knew. The blood was nothing to do with him, so he carried on with his business.

After reading what I've written about the people I spend my life investigating, it might not come as a surprise to learn that I'm not particularly tolerant. When new members join my team, the others say to them, 'When you want to tell Mark something, just get straight to the point.' I absorb so much information, I haven't got time to listen to waffle. I'm wrong about this in many ways – I know that. A lot of people like talking, and sometimes I need to give them that opportunity. Sometimes I think I could live on a desert island, though – on my own, quiet, not having to cope with anybody. But then I'd miss my family so that wouldn't work.

I like to weigh up people. I listen to every word they say. I may be terrible with names, but tell me some detail or other – even in an offhand way – and I'll pick up on that and remember it. The ways people say those little things can also make a big difference; it can happen subconsciously, but it's true, they've said what they really mean. That's why I study people all the time. Some people give away a lot of their secrets easily – the loud way they talk, their clothes and the bags they carry, the glances they make when they think no one's looking. I'd like to say I can read people and tell you things about them but that's tricky. What I can do is observe, and keep logging in my mind what I see.

That's the training. During an investigation, it's amazing what you're able to find out about someone's personal life – what they've done that they think no one will ever know about. The police always know that in any major inquiry they will always solve other, more minor crimes. Say there's been a murder. When the police start looking into the crime, they'll canvas the neighbours and discover a burglary took place near by. They'll need to investigate that in case it turns out the burglars are also the killers. More people get drawn into the investigation and more things are learned, good and bad.

People are at the heart of everything I do. There's always a victim and they usually have a family that needs supporting. If I ever need reminding of this I take a look at the day's emails and post; I get so many approaches from the general public asking for my help. When I'm not on the TV, then I get about one or two enquiries a week, but when there's a programme such as *The Investigator* on regularly, then I'm likely to get between twenty and thirty emails a week, all from people desperate to have someone help them with their case.

Some cases are at a point where I feel that to take them on would be an almost impossible feat, that I would expect to fail if I did. The disappearance of Claudia Lawrence (who went missing in York in 2009; there has been no sign of her since then, and no one knows what has happened to her) is one that I believe has reached a dead-end at the moment, though I don't think it's unsolvable. If you were able to apply certain investigative techniques (not all of them completely legal), and had an unlimited amount of money, you could find something out. I think a number of people were responsible for her disappearance and her murder. They know who they are, and they're walking amongst us. If enough pressure was applied, you could probably get the answer there.

The abduction of Madeleine McCann is, however, one I'd put into the unsolvable category. I believe Madeleine was the victim of an opportunistic criminal whose act was random – she wandered out of the apartment and into the path of this person. The case hasn't been solved simply because a crucial CCTV camera was turned off, meaning that whoever took Madeleine was not identifiable at the scene. I'd love to think there could be an end to the case – that either Madeleine is returned to Gerry, Kate, Sean and Amelie or there is some kind of resolution in terms of someone being convicted for the offence. The sad reality is, this far on, the likelihood of Madeleine being alive now is incredibly slim. Unfortunately, in almost every case of stranger child abduction, within the space of twenty-four hours the child is dead. When older children or teenagers are abducted, the victims can be kept alive (sometimes for many years) and are found or escape. If the abduction is sexually motivated or trafficking is involved, there is long-term value to a paedophile or trafficker in a teenager. An offender can reason with a teenager, but not with a three-year-old.

Having this sort of stuff swirling inside my head can make me a difficult person to be around. There's a mental strength I need to possess to be in this line of work, where I'm having to hold together many strands of an investigation – indeed, many investigations – at the same time. I juggle so many different cases at once, all at different stages, that one might go on the back burner while another requires my attention, and then I'll switch them round to focus on something else. Of course, there are often issues that can take a bit longer to untangle or resolve because you have to involve other people, and it becomes a slower process because of that.

When I'm working with my producer, Lesley, or somebody else such as David Wells, I'll share things with them, thoughts or otherwise. I do think it's important to get somebody else's point of view – I'll always listen to another take on how to get around a problem or see a route through to solving an issue.

I've always loved a challenge. If I'm told that I can't do something, that makes me want to take a closer look and say, 'I bet I can.' I'm still learning, of course, and I don't rest on my laurels – I'm only as good as my last programme, my last investigation. To do the sort of job I do it's necessary to have that drive to meet a challenge, that passion, that commitment. It's also about giving an air of confidence; I know what I'm doing, I know where I want to get to, and to make sure the team do too I have to convince them first. I always say to them exactly what I always say to my clients: I won't always get there but I'll do all I can to try to.

That desire to meet challenges and take on the more difficult jobs probably increases the chances of not always getting an answer for my client. This is my biggest problem; I struggle enormously with failure. If I set out to do something and don't get an end result, I feel like I've failed. I beat myself up over it. Even if I've managed to progress a case further forward than it's ever been before and I've given the family some answers – or at the very least found them a voice when they'd given up on thinking anyone would ever listen to them again – I do take any kind of failure especially hard.

My motivations aren't financial; if it was about the money then I wouldn't do what I do. As I've said before, I help far too many people to be able to make lots of money, because for some cases I absorb a lot of the costs myself. I pay travel expenses to some places out of my own pocket – such as crime scenes, to see for myself what the site looked like. I absorb costs like that because I know I have a profile, and the ability to investigate crimes; if I can get people answers when they've been let down, why wouldn't I try?

Take the case of Jessie Earl. When I met her parents, Valerie and John, they'd not spoken to the media for ten years. 'We're not doing any more interviews,' they said to me when I first made contact. After talking to them on the phone, I went on my own to see them, and we spoke for a while. I asked them to think about what I'd proposed we did about their case and they immediately said, 'We don't need to think about it, you've sat here and completely convinced us, and we want to work with you.'

I recognize what a privilege this is, to have become part of their lives, in some way. It's important that I remain objective, of course, but we also started to form a bond. I want to succeed for them; that's how it works. I want to give a voice to people such as the Earls; the longer the absence of their loved one goes on, the more they get forgotten. For many families, keeping their son or daughter's name in the public domain is the only way they have to make sure that that doesn't happen. Who's going to review a murder file from 1975 when they're dealing with so many more pressing current ones?

I've always found that taking a break from thinking about a specific problem in a case is amazing because when I come back to it, somehow the solution (or *a* solution) presents itself. I expect the people I work with, both my team and my clients, to feel the same – it's important to give the case a break, sometimes even for a month, and come back to it. That pause can allow everyone to see things differently.

One of the issues most of my clients struggle with is wanting the case resolved immediately; understandably so, when often it's been weighing on them for a long time. The mere fact I've got involved sometimes means they believe I'll solve it straight away, that I can make a programme about their case within a few days. It's not as simple as that, I explain. Take the case of Matthew Green; he was missing for six years before he was back in the UK seeing his parents. Things take time and have to happen that way.

I explain to the people I work with that it's helpful for them to feel the same way I do: that you have to believe you'll find a resolution to a case, and if things appear to have ground to a halt, something will happen to move them along again. I do the job because I live in hope that one day someone will come forward with that vital piece of information, that clue about where someone's body has been hidden, for example. There might be someone out there about to reach the age of seventy, or maybe eighty, someone on whom this secret has weighed heavily throughout their life, who thinks, 'I've kept this secret for so long, I need to pass it on before I die.' There must be many people in jail who, with the right motivation, could tell the families or the police something – especially as they get closer to their own death.

On that subject, I believe that a life sentence should mean life in jail. That isn't always clear; however long a sentence is, the parameters seem to change once someone's spent time inside. I accept that the sentence served has to revolve around the offender and the nature of their crime, but it can't just be about them – how remorseful they are, what they've sought to do during their time as an inmate, what their behaviour has been like in jail. It has to reflect society's distaste for their offence and, most importantly of all, what the victims of the crime, or their families, feel – would they feel safe with the perpetrator out on parole? In that sense, I suppose the length of time served depends on what the impact of the crime they committed was.

This must be why Stuart Hazell received such a phenomenal sentence. He will be seventy-five before he's even considered for parole, if he lives that long. Tony Holland, too, got a remarkable sentence: thirty-five years. I know that at times it puzzles the police, never mind the public, as to why some killers get shorter terms – eight years, say – while others might get nearly four decades. It's hard to know why the disparity occurs. Initially, I was shocked at the sentence for Hazell – other cases I'd seen, involving higher levels of brutality, resulted in shorter sentences – but then I thought about it, and I could see all the aggravating factors that had contributed to such a tough sentence. Hazell had concealed Tia Sharp's body in the family home; he'd denied his crime; some incredibly serious sexual offences of a macabre nature had been committed; he was connected to her – considered a family member, even; it was clearly premeditated; and he kept up this pretence of being a grieving relative to torment the people he lived with.

While I have no problem with Hazell being sent away for life, I want his time inside to be productive. Not because I care about him, but because there are people in prison who could benefit from a regime inside that reduces the risk of violence and therefore makes rehabilitation for them, and for the general public, easier. Hazell will never be released, but everyone inside should be doing something worthwhile. I wouldn't even jail most of the people currently inside, anyway, the non-violent offenders; how many present an immediate risk? Far better for them to be serving sentences within the community, doing things to benefit that community, than being locked away with hardened criminals. Often, people are surprised to hear me talking like this, but I've never been one to toe the party line, and I think if you want to alter policing so that we police to the vulnerable, as I've previously spoken about, then the justice system as a whole should act in the same way. Additionally, prisons are full of people with mental health conditions, addictions and learning difficulties; I'm not saying that makes those inmates any less culpable, but if we treat them in the same way as offenders such as Hazell, Holland and Peter Tobin, then we are not helping them prepare for the day they rejoin society, and that can only be a bad thing.

I do believe we have the best criminal justice system in the world, but there is one gaping flaw in it: juries. If there is a dominant foreperson, they will take all the other people with them – in both a positive and negative way. We seem to regard the privacy of a jury room as sacrosanct, which makes the process a hidden one. Has social media, the internet, damaged the way juries vote? Who knows – we cannot ask juries questions, as that's regarded as an obstruction of justice. Similarly, are our judges completely immune to being influenced by the world around them; can they be truly impartial? To be so, especially in a high-profile case, would mean not being allowed to watch the news, or listen to the radio, or read the newspapers, or talk to their colleagues. They shouldn't go online, or use social media. That's the judges, too – never mind the juries. Would that sort of seclusion ever happen? No – which is why I think they can be influenced, even if they don't think they can be.

For me, all my work comes back to the same starting point. It's always been about the impact of crime on the families, the innocent. They didn't ask to get drawn into someone's offences, and often the families of the perpetrator are as oblivious to those crimes as the victim's family. I've always found that to be one of the biggest challenges I have to handle: being in possession of information that's going to change someone's life, just prior to it happening, as when I saw Max Clifford on breakfast TV. When I have that information, I keep it confidential, to myself; but I've always found that it weighs heavily on me. Particularly when it's going to turn someone's life upside down and result in their children or their partner likely never having anything to do with them again. This is someone who has committed an especially horrific crime which they've kept secret, so I have no sympathy for them, of course. But when I'm stood outside their house, at 5 a.m., ready to bang on the door and ask my questions, whether as a policeman or as a journalist, I will often think of their family and how I'm about to upend their world.

It's always good to be reminded of how powerful the police (and not just the force, but individual officers) can be, as they can change someone's life. From time to time they need to be reminded of that. It does happen that a number of offenders will commit suicide when they're being investigated, sometimes before there's even been a charge, let alone a conviction. It's sad when that happens, because there are always other people left behind. And not just their own family, but those people who are left wanting to know the truth about what happened to their loved one in their final hours.

There's a commonly held view that the families of

offenders always know what their relative is up to. That's not been proved to be the case, and while there are certainly times when you'd think they had to know, surely, the evidence does back that up. Cunning killers such as Peter Tobin compartmentalize. Angus Sinclair, too. His wife said, 'I'd never got it – the police in particular said, "You must have got it." But I had no idea, I thought he was a womanizer, I thought he was out having affairs. We fell out a few times over that, but I never thought for one minute he was going to kill somebody.'

It's easier to live that kind of life – one where you show different faces to different people – if you're able to act like a normal person. Angus Sinclair had the ability to be liked; so too, at least away from home, did Fred West. Nobody liked Peter Tobin – he was, and is, generally considered a vile man. It's a shame that, before he died in March 2019, Sinclair never told the truth about what he did. I don't think Tobin ever will. I think he'll carry his secrets to the grave, but Sinclair, if he'd lived, might have been persuaded to speak. So many people in jail must be willing to open up about what they did, in the right circumstances, but once someone is in jail, who's interested in spending the time and the effort involved to make that happen?

Recently, I've started to look at gathering information together for the kind of database that doesn't exist in the UK, a complete catalogue of all unsolved murders across the country. Shockingly, one that covers the national picture has never been compiled – there is no central collection point for data relating to unsolved murders. Working with a researcher, I've so far amassed details of over 2,300 unsolved killings committed in the UK since 1900, I'm setting up a website called Unsolved Cases. The purpose being to create an interactive map of the UK, with a page (and, over time, a short video covering each case) for each murder.

The value of such a site is immediately apparent in helping to identify a number of murders as linked. Police forces have never managed to connect these cases because of the constraints on their time and money, and because they have lacked the kind of central point that our website will soon provide.

At the moment, I'm funding the construction of this website myself, so that the information we gather can be shared with police forces who might be in a position to act once they can see the greater picture. And it's why I've written this book – to help with that funding. With new intelligence, I'm hopeful that we'll be able to help solve some of these hitherto unsolved crimes and bring some hope to loved ones that they will see justice done.

The launch of the website will take place soon. There are so many cases to collate and prepare

information for, but I remain passionate about helping to solve some of these historic crimes and about
locating people (or, if it comes to it, their remains) lost
to their families. To bring what has been hidden into
the light.

Ursula Herrmann, aged ten, was cycling home through woods near her home in Eching, Germany on 15 September 1981 when she was abducted. She was then put into a box measuring only one and a half metres deep and a metre wide, and found dead from asphyxiation two weeks later.

Fifteen-year-old Lee Boxell was last seen on 18 September 1988 in Sutton High Street, London. No trace of him has ever been found and nobody has been charged in connection with his disappearance. New evidence has now emerged that sheds greater light on what happened to him.

Art student Jessie Earl was aged twenty-two when she disappeared in May 1980 from her home in the seaside town of Eastbourne, East Sussex. Her skeletal remains were found hidden in undergrowth on Beachy Head in March 1989.

Louise Kay was last seen in 1988 in Sussex, having dropped off her friend in her distinctive Ford Fiesta after a night out. Neither Louise nor her car have ever been found; I have linked one man to her disappearance and murder.

Fourteen-year-old Sarah Benford was last seen in Kettering, Northamptonshire in April 2000. Her disappearance was not initially treated as murder, but new evidence now shines a light on the sexual exploitation and grooming of girls in the area.

Schoolgirl Tia Sharp was murdered in 2012 by Stuart Hazell, her grandmother's partner. At his Old Bailey trial Hazell was sentenced to life, with a minimum term of thirty-eight years.

ACKNOWLEDGEMENTS

I always knew that writing a book was never going to be an easy task – after all, I have dyslexia, which means that my construction of sentences and paragraphs is very poor. This is probably why I have focused on working in TV, telling a story or showing an investigation visually, rather than in print. Those who know me would probably describe me as a pretty quiet, deep person, who keeps much to himself. During my career I have been entrusted with many secrets and so I tend to give very little away. Idle gossip is not for me; clear detail and straight to the point is how I work. That said, I have found writing this book very rewarding and quite cathartic. My heartfelt thanks, therefore, to Humphrey Price for his invaluable help in crafting what I hope is a compelling read, and for his calming influence and patience. Also, to my editor, Michelle Signore, who has been a delight to work with – kind, sincere and sharp as a knife; to the staff at Transworld Publishers and, of course, my book agent Eugenie Furnuss from 42MP. Without all of you, this book would have just remained an idea.

Of course, none of what I have achieved over the years would have been possible without the nurturing love and support of my mum and dad, my wife and my three amazing children. Getting a work-life balance has always been hard, and my dedication to help others has sometimes meant that I have neglected those closest to me. I am immensely proud of my children as they begin adult life. My two girls are both following careers in engineering and my son is about to start university, where he will study sports rehabilitation. It has always been my family that has pulled me through, even at the darkest of times. The work I do brings incredible highs, such as getting a breakthrough on a case, or catching a suspect; but it also brings real lows, such as not getting the answers I need to solve a case or attacks from the tiny number of people who are protecting offenders.

Throughout our childhood and adult life, we meet people who have a direct impact on helping to shape our future, both as a person and in our chosen career. Two such people were my junior-school headmaster, the late Dominic Spencer, and my senior-school house-master at Pierrepont School, Mr Kirk. Dominic was a large and charismatic man, who was always incredibly happy and had a positive outlook on life. It was under his watch at junior school that I got the bug for rugby and I was very fortunate in being able to play at a good level at both Harlequins and Surrey. Whilst playing in the Middlesex 7s at Twickenham in front of a crowd of around 60,000, I even scored a try! At Pierrepont, Mr Kirk had the control and presence of an army sergeant major. His influence and support during my teenage years certainly helped to nurture and guide me.

Rugby has always been a central part of my life and remains so today. The team building and discipline is something that I believe could help guide many young people, particularly those who experience difficult times in their lives. Bill Deighton, my junior Surrey school coach, was a teacher at City of London Free-men's School and was a straight-talking man. He constantly pushed me to be a better player and to under-stand teamwork; I owe him a lot. Also, thanks to my coach at Guildford and Godalming Rugby Club (now known as Guildford Rugby Club) Dave Hodgkiss, and at senior Surrey level, the late Dr Des Carroll.

I also owe a great deal to my career in the police, which was instrumental in shaping me into the person I am today. Being a police officer gave me the skills and tradecraft to be an investigative reporter and the robustness to stand up to intimidation and threats from the people I seek to expose. During my probation I was stationed at Guildford police station in Surrey. My sergeant, Nick Overton, was a gruff man, whom many other officers feared. He was pedantic and not one to suffer fools gladly. He would inspect all my reports and files with a fine-tooth comb and, when working earlies on a Sunday, would have me learning definitions and rules of evidence. At the time, his approach was not something that I appreciated, but he taught me so much. It is thanks to him that I am as professional and thorough as I am today. So, thank you Nick.

It is said that a true friend is one who sticks around when the going gets tough, and that is so right. My lack of trust in people and the work that I do means that my inner circle is very small. Aged eleven, at junior school, I formed a friendship with Andrew Warry, now a professional tennis coach. To this day, he remains one of the few close friends I have. Another, whom I have known for over thirty years, is James Ford – he and I used to go drinking in the pubs of Farnham when we were seventeen. In more recent years: Sky tennis correspondent and professional tennis coach Mark Petchey, my former police colleague detective sergeant Kevin Suckling, Mike Cohen – an incredible watchmaker from Bellagio Global, and my close friend and work colleague solicitor David Wells. Finally, two truly genuine people, John and Jan, who have provided security and support for me on so many jobs and have become close friends – I am no Donald Trump, but they really would take a bullet for me.

To those who have helped guide my career as an investigative reporter: in particular, the former editor of ITV's *Tonight*, Mike Lewis, who gave me my first break as a reporter, and the past and present editors of ITV's *This Morning*, Pete Ogden and Martin Frizell.

Most of my television work has been with ITV and I am very grateful for the chances that I was given by the former director of television Peter Fincham and the continued support and opportunities given to me by the current director of television, Kevin Lygo.

Any good leader will tell you that it is the quality of the team that creates success and as such I must single out my TV partner and producer Lesley Gardiner, and assistant producer Rebecca Hogarth. They are both incredible people and I have learned so much from them. I also owe much to, and have great respect for, two executives: former managing director of Shiver, Alexander Gardiner, and the former editor of BBC *Panorama* and now ITV commissioner, Tom Giles. Both are incredibly talented individuals who have believed in me and provided me with a huge amount of support.

I have written for many of the national newspapers, but have formed a special relationship with one – the *Mirror*. Being a newspaper journalist can be a tough job and, like all jobs, there are very good and very bad journalists. The *Mirror* and its staff truly represent what is good about the British national press. In particular, the *Mirror*'s editors Lloyd Embley and Gary Jones, reporter Dominic Herbert and journalists Andy Gardiner and Mike Hamilton, all of whom are a true credit to the profession.

Thanks also to Simon Cowell. Between us, we created the format for the crime series *The Investigator*. I have got to know Simon well and not only has he been a great support to me, but also to my family. Contrary to his bad-boy TV image, he is one of the nicest and kindest people I have ever met. He has a true heart of gold, and what he does to help people behind the scenes makes him a very special person and someone I am proud to know.

I am very grateful for the dedication and support given to me by my agents over the years. My past agents Sylvia Tidy-Harris from STH Management and Holly Bott from James Grant, and my current agents Keith Bishop and Sam Kane from KBA Talent and the effervescent Zoie Wainwright.

As well as my TV work I have seen how other media can play a vital role in bringing attention to criminal investigations, and to maximize this I have recently teamed up with the incredibly smart Paul Blanchard from Right Angles Global to start making a new crime podcast series.

I must also praise the professionalism and integrity of the many police officers both past and present who have helped – and continue to help – me investigate and bring attention to unsolved cases, thereby helping victims' families and loved ones get answers.

And a special mention to my dedicated PA, Nikki Aldersalde. I am sure she could never have imagined what she was taking on when she started working for me. Her dedication, amazing support, professionalism and ability to organize me helps to make my incredibly complicated life much more manageable.

ABOUT THE AUTHOR

Mark Williams-Thomas is an investigative reporter. His many awards include two Royal Television Society Awards, a Broadcasting Press Guild Award and an International Peabody Award. He is also BAFTA nominated. A former police detective, he has reported on nearly all of the biggest crime stories of the last decade. It was Mark's *Exposure* documentary that finally revealed Jimmy Savile as one of the nation's most prolific paedophiles; as a result of his investigation, the Metropolitan Police set up Operation Yewtree. Mark now has his own ITV prime-time crime show, *The Investigator*, and presents the *Unsolved* strand on *This Morning*, looking at unsolved crimes.